D0394528

Daddy's
Little
G⚽alie

Daddy's *Little* G⚽alie

A Father, His Daughters, and Sports

ROBERT STRAUSS

Andrews McMeel Publishing, LLC
Kansas City • Sydney • London

Daddy's Little Goalie copyright © 2011 by Robert Strauss. All rights reserved. Printed in the United States of America. No part of this book may be used or reproduced in any manner whatsoever without written permission except in the case of reprints in the context of reviews.

Andrews McMeel Publishing, LLC
an Andrews McMeel Universal company
1130 Walnut Street, Kansas City, Missouri 64106

www.andrewsmcmeel.com

11 12 13 14 15 MLT 10 9 8 7 6 5 4 3 2 1

ISBN: 978-1-4494-0234-1

Library of Congress Control Number: 2010930553

ATTENTION: SCHOOLS AND BUSINESSES
Andrews McMeel books are available at quantity discounts with bulk purchase for educational, business, or sales promotional use. For information, please e-mail the Andrews McMeel Publishing Special Sales Department: specialsales@amuniversal.com

To my mom and dad, Edna and Sam, who never got to see the girls but have always been watching over them

Contents

Introduction: Not Just Rickety-Rack Anymore, Dad. . ix

Girls Do Play Sports 1

The Biddie Sports Quadrangle:
Soccer, Swim and Dive, Softball, and Basketball 13

Getting Serious 27

From A to B and Back Again:
The Agony of the Too-Soon Tryout 41

Sporting Transitions: The Last Innocent Years 57

High School: A Lot of Sweet and a Bit of Bitter 71

Whoa, There's a Mom Here, Too 85

Intensity and the Nonsports Experience:
Competitiveness Doesn't Stop Off the Court Either . . 97

The Denouement:
Recruiting, Reflection, and Retrenchment 111

What Have We Learned? Where Will We Go? 127

Not Just Rickety-Rack Anymore, Dad

To call the Haddonfield Memorial High School gym venerable, or any other positive modifier, would be generous. It is not quite squalid, but perhaps it runs more toward dank and seedy. No matter how many bond issue upgrades the school district puts into the lighting, it always seems too dim. The bleachers are ill-spaced, making sitting through even one period a leg-wrenching experience. There are allegedly insulated windows right below the inefficient heat blowers. Spectators can be too hot on one side of their bodies and still have damp, frigid streaks running up their backs.

The scorer's table is installed so that the bare wood bleacher behind it is too far away for the clock operator to reach the buttons or for the scorer to even see over the railing down to the part of the floor where substitutes check in, which aggravates coaches, players, and referees because it causes them to miss crucial substitutions.

In the rafters and along the walls are banners indicating the array of championships Haddonfield High athletes have won. The banners are speckled with mold and dust, but they are real. For more than thirty years in a row, Haddonfield has won the

Colonial Conference all-sports crown. It could be even more, but the banners reach back only to 1969–70, enough, presumably, being enough. In the mid-2000s, the Shop Rite supermarket chain started giving an annual award to the school with the best overall sports record in each of New Jersey's four school population size categories. Haddonfield has won in Group II by wide margins every year, and the space on the west wall is running out for those large banners.

To visitors, the effect is galling because Haddonfield is the richest town around and could easily afford all sorts of fanciness. To locals, though, it is a bit of endearing familiarity and coziness, as if *Hoosiers II* could be set right there and Gene Hackman could come trundling in to coach. Good numbers of Haddonfielders are second-, third-, and who-knows-how-far-back generation residents. The town allegedly dates to the buying of the land in the 1680s by Englishman John Haddon, who later sent his daughter, Elizabeth, to settle it. Lizzie, as she is affectionately known to every schoolkid in town, probably shot hoops in the ancient Haddonfield High gym.

On either side of the scoreboard are slats for letters or numbers to be pushed in. On the left side of the scoreboard are the names of that year's boys' basketball players, with their numbers from smallest to largest going down the column. On the right, it is a similar run of girls. Every day for a year, the kids lucky enough to make the varsity have their names on display for every gym class, every dance, every graduation, every game; the main school events taking place in the gym, bleak and endearing as it is to residents.

In December 2007, my wife and I shivered in anticipation of the first home girls' basketball game. Would our older daughter, Ella, be on the board? She had had a decent freshman year, starting most games as the 5-foot-zip shooting guard. Now, though, she was a sophomore, clearly secure on junior varsity. But how high on the varsity food chain? We tried to remember how many slats there were on the right side of the scoreboard. Were there 12? 14? 10? We were too embarrassed by our concern to ask anyone or even be caught sneaking into the gym to look. We would just have to wait until opening night.

The junior varsity games at Haddonfield start at 5:30 P.M., and no one is there but JV parents and a few teachers and close friends. Even with regular conference crowns, many South Jersey winners, and occasional state championships on the varsity, JV games are as much family affairs as a great aunt's birthday bash.

Still, we were pumped. We walked through the double glass doors of the faded and chipped brick building and on past the zillions of trophies dating back seemingly several millennia in smudged glass cases lining the hallway. We ducked into the gym and started up the stairs to the middle range of stands, not looking back over our shoulders at the scoreboard, fearing, like Lot's wife, that we would turn into unlucky pillars of salt if we gazed too prematurely.

We got to a good place at the top row—the stands go about fifteen rows up a steep ridge—because we knew we would need seats with a straight back for a JV–varsity doubleheader. My wife and I breathed hard and turned ourselves to the scoreboard.

Like a beacon on a hillside, like the big old smoking Camel cigarette billboard that defined mid-twentieth-century Times Square, like the biggest jackpot sign in the biggest casino in Vegas, there at the top of the right side of the scoreboard read, in capital letters, "3 STRAUSS."

We each maniacally took several photographs. Sylvia, our seventh grader, rolled her eyes almost violently.

"You are definitely nuts," she said more than once.

My wife, though, looked at me as she probably hadn't since our first date.

"You could die right now, couldn't you?" was all she had to say.

In 1970–71, two years after I graduated high school and the first year after the passage of Title IX, the federal law that demanded that women and girls be granted the same rights in athletics as men and boys, the National Association of High Schools determined that 294,000 American girls were playing high school sports. That paltry number, the association said, was probably twice what it had been a decade earlier. By 2008–09, when my older daughter, Ella, was a junior in high school and my younger one, Sylvia, was in eighth grade, more than 3 million girls were playing sports in American high schools. Since Title IX's inception, boys' participation increased by about 20 percent to five million, less than the rate of high school attendance in general. As the stats show, girls had created a whole new universe.

Not only that, but what they were doing was far different. In 1971, girls in New Jersey, where I grew up, and in many other states, were playing six-girl basketball. Two girls played offense, two played defense, and only two played both ends, presumably because girls didn't have the stamina boys did to all make it up and down the court. They wore uniforms that looked like bloomers. Girls' lacrosse developed with one more player on the field than the boys and rules that prohibited any blocking or hitting, to prevent the delicate young ladies from getting hurt. Girls played softball—again with ten players in the field instead of nine—pitching underhanded with shorter baselines and bigger balls that couldn't go as hard or as far as boys' baseballs. Even with these truncated versions of boys' sports, most girls playing sports in American high schools did swimming, running, gymnastics, or tennis, not contact sports. When I got to Carleton College, I played freshman basketball and club rugby. Despite the gender equity rising on that liberal campus, women didn't have freshman basketball, and they were not allowed to play in the intramural softball league, slow-pitch as it was.

Today, at least a couple of girls play in the Haddonfield Little League with the boys every year. Nobody questions how hard girls smack each other in soccer and basketball (five-on-five these days, to be sure), and black-and-blue marks caused by errant—or intentionally fierce—lacrosse sticks are common prom sights. Carleton has been a national power in recent years in women's rugby.

My girls grew up in a town 2 miles away from my childhood home among houses that look just as grand today as they did to me as a kid, but their idea of what girls can do in sports has taken a trajectory unimagined by their female predecessors in those houses just a generation ago.

About half the kids, both boys and girls, at Haddonfield Memorial High School play varsity sports. The town is sports-crazed but probably no more than most towns around, and the sports pages of all the local papers, although they may somewhat favor football and boys' basketball, are never hesitant to lead with stories about girls' athletics. Haddonfield cleaves to its no-cut policy, one of the pleasant remnants of its Quaker past, which increases those participation numbers, but its success rate says that even the benchwarmers are pretty good. In 2009–10, it won an astounding seven Group II (midsized schools) state championships and came in second or third in four more sports.

So it is hardly a surprise that Ella and Sylvia would want to be a part of that milieu. There have been wonderful arts successes in Haddonfield's history. Michael Landon (né Eugene Orowitz) did his first acting as a teenager at Haddonfield Plays and Players. Steven Spielberg had a Haddonfield address during junior high, when his father worked nearby, and he said he was inspired to do *Schindler's List* by memories of being a Jewish kid in a decidedly non-Jewish community, as Haddonfield was in those days. The *Halloween* movies take place in fictional "Haddonfield, Illinois," because one of the producers, Debra Hill, grew up in town.

Still, the arts tend to be in the background here, and even the student actors and singers usually play at least one sport or at least revel in being in the marching band at football games. Strangely enough, those football games are not as well attended as they might be because often the other teams are playing their own games on those fall Fridays. In Ella's years at Haddonfield Memorial, three of the four homecoming queens were field hockey captains and one was a Division I college recruit soccer defender—not a pom-pom girl or beauty pageant moll in sight.

For much of my early career, I was a sportswriter or TV sports producer and, for a time, the baseball and college basketball reporter for *Sports Illustrated*. In my twenties, I was a correspondent for a nascent magazine, *WomenSports*, considering myself a bit of a feminist. Still, when the doctor told me in the delivery room the morning of October 4, 1991, that I had a beautiful baby girl, I hesitated just a breath and said, "Well, okay." It was pretty much the same on January 20, 1995, when Sylvia was born. I was ready for a Sam, to be named after my father.

We weren't going to go for three. I always had ready the sporting line that we were going to stick with "man-to-man child-rearing and not go to zone." So girls were it. Hey, I always liked girls. I had dated them for about twenty years and had married a good one, midwestern stock from Dearborn, Michigan. It was going to be fine. I still had my sports pages, my noon pickup basketball games, and maybe a Friday night high school football game on occasion.

Living in the head of a 1960s sports guy, though, I still was not prepared for what was to come.

Girls Do Play Sports

Lwent to my first Phillies game in mid-July 1957. It was only a week or two after my sixth birthday, and I was already a diligent fan, memorizing and calculating batting averages and earned-run averages and spelling even difficult ethnic names of players such as Rip Repulski, Ray Semproch, Stan Lopata, and the immortal Go-Go Chico Fernández.

Ella was just about that age when she curled up with me on the couch one night as I was idly watching a Philadelphia 76ers game. My ardor for sports watching had cooled over the years, but I still felt a bit of a connoisseur. I was one of the lucky boys to become a professional sportswriter. I had worked as a small-town columnist, as a TV sports producer, and even as a reporter for a year at *Sports Illustrated*. Sportswriters, and especially ex-sportswriters, as I was by that point, can be a cynical lot. They watch games and comment on the nuances of the athletics but then grumble about overpaid athletes and long road trips and the lack of appreciation by those writers and editors in news and business and features, who considered themselves "real" journalists. Sports is the sandbox; news is Valhalla.

I didn't think much about this as Ella curled up. I just put my left arm around her and let out a good kind of sigh. We watched silently for a minute or two, the Sixers and their opponents doing a host of insignificant things. Then Ella, still looking at the screen, asked me in a clear, bright tone one of those inevitable five-year-old-daughter questions:

"Daddy, why is it that only boys play sports?"

I shot upward on the couch like a crazed animal, my arm knocking Ella forward almost to the floor.

"Well, no. No, girls play sports. Not only boys. Girls. Yes, girls play," I babbled, but then I shuddered with the thought, "Don't they? I mean, they must."

Ella was satisfied with my answer and curled back in. I was disturbed, though. I think it was the second quarter of the game, and I don't remember seeing a basket clearly the rest of the way. Ella fell asleep about fifteen minutes after her question, but I couldn't stop thinking about it.

This is not hyperbole. I really was disturbed. When I was growing up in the 1950s and 1960s, girls really didn't play sports—at least not with us. Even fourth-grade kickball was a manly-man kind of thing. I broke my wrist trying to catch a huge kickball pop-up by Ronnie Eckert, one of the biggest and toughest kids in the class. Would you send a girl out on a mission like that? That would have been about 1960. Did women even have the vote then?

I dragged Ella up to her bed and took the sports section of the day's paper out of the recycling bag. I ripped a couple of pages trying to find the local sports section and finally found it. Even when I was at my first job at the *Mankato Free Press*, the daily paper for the largest town, such as it was, in southwestern Minnesota, I was never inclined to read even the stories I wrote about local sports. Mankato was the preseason training center for the Minnesota Vikings, so any chance I got to write about that, or at least the Mankato State University teams, I did so. I even volunteered to cover the football games of tiny Gustavus Adolphus College, a few dozen miles down the road, once getting the privilege of an all-expenses-paid trip to Sioux Falls, South Dakota, to cover the Gustavus Adolphus–Augustana game.

So when I took to perusing the *Philadelphia Inquirer*'s New Jersey high school sports coverage, I did so with trepidation. Nonetheless, deep down in the agate-sized type, I could make out that there would be a girls' basketball game in the next town the next evening: Haddonfield would be playing Haddon Heights, and Ella and I would be going, damn it.

Girls would be playing sports.

It was cold, and Ella was well bundled as we trudged from the car the next night into the Haddon Heights gym. Ella pined for a soft pretzel, a Philadelphia delicacy, especially slathered with mustard over the large granules of salt seemingly pasted on top. I acquiesced and then saw the sign in nearly foot-high letters saying, "No Food or Drink in Gym." The game was about to start, but the pretzel was taking priority. Even though I was practically pretzel-phobic, I ripped off a piece and shoved it in my mouth to make it go faster. I was still a sportswriter at heart: You go to a game for the game. Mascots, food, halftime shootouts, exploding scoreboards, huge foam hands with pointed fingers, that's all for the hoi polloi. The game is the thing.

Well, maybe not, I discovered, for a five-year-old. The opening horn had sounded and the pretzel was still half eaten. I peered in the door, looking back every so often at the pretzel progress. The Haddonfield girls seemed quite good. They could pass and make a shot or two from 15 feet. This wasn't going to be too painful. I was a basketball junkie, playing pickup whenever I could, sometimes six or seven days a week, and some of these girls looked almost good enough to play in our manic full-court games.

It was midway through the first quarter when Ella burped and pronounced herself ready to walk in. I took a smudge of mustard off her parka and, hand in hand, we were off into our first girls' sporting event. We bounded up to the top of the stands at midcourt.

"Best seats in the house," I announced to her, though I was a bit disappointed that we were at a game where we could actually get the best seats in the house in the middle of the first quarter. I was getting pretty dubious about girls' sports.

Ella, though, was enthralled. Not at the game, to be sure, but at the Haddonfield Bulldog mascot. Actually, Haddonfield's mascot is spelled Bulldawg and is thin, long, and gray, unlike any Bulldog or Bulldawg I had ever seen. I had become inured to mascots, I thought, having survived watching the most obnoxious of the breed, the similarly spell-check-challenged Phillie Phanatic, as a sportswriter and spectator. The Phanatic is green and oversized, with a big stomach, bug eyes, and a tubular snout. It makes somewhat sexual gestures, like putting its hands on its rear and pushing the big stomach forward. It is some kind of animal, I guess, but mostly just obnoxious. Kids love it, and they would rather wave to it than watch the game, which no doubt rankled me as a purist even more.

Now my daughter was enthralled with a Bulldawg rather than watching sixteen-year-old girls, presumably from the neighborhood, loft a few. The quarter break then brought on the cheerleaders. I never quite understood cheerleaders. Even in the era of hip-hop cheers and rhythmic stomping, they always seemed to have their timing off. They led cheers when no one was listening or, most often, got in the way of players actually trying to do something near the sidelines. In football, at least they were off the side in a big field and I could ignore them. In basketball, they were unavoidably in sight range. Furthermore, it seemed like there might have been all of forty or fifty people in the stands, presumably at least half of them rooting for Haddon Heights, so the dozen or so Haddonfield cheerleaders could have each had a fan or two of their own.

Fortunately, a few minutes of Bulldawg watching was enough. Cheerleaders didn't excite her. I didn't have a rah-rah babe, and I was happy. Ella now did her cuddle up with me and looked intently at the basketball girls. When one in a Haddonfield uniform made a shot, she didn't immediately cheer, but she moved her right hand up and outward in a shooting motion. She continued this for a few minutes at halftime.

"Daddy, I want to do that. I will learn," she said. I was tempted to offer another pretzel as a reward for those words as we went out in the hall for a potty stop, but I merely puffed my chest out in admiration.During the second half, the Haddonfield girls began to crush Haddon Heights. Twenty points soon became forty, while the Heights girls—the Lady Garnets, as if stones had gender—stayed haplessly in single digits.

"We're winning. We're winning. We're winning," Ella screeched as she continued her shooting motion, getting closer to perfect, even with a follow-through, at every moment.

As the fourth quarter moved onward, it became a bit embarrassing. Haddonfield's scrubbinis were now annihilating their opponents. With the score about 58–12, I could no longer bear Ella's cheers, oblivious as she was to the impropriety of huzzahs during a wipeout.

"We have to leave," I said, throwing her parka at her.

"Why? Isn't it wonderful? Aren't we winning? Can't we stay?" she pleaded.

I couldn't. The first lesson I had to teach was sportsmanship. She tromped out to the car, a bit unhappy.

"Why can't we score as much as we can?" she asked earnestly.

"Sometimes you sort of go backwards," I said. "Sometimes the more you score, the more you lose."

She hugged my leg.

"Don't worry, Daddy," she said. "I won't ever lose."

I was stunned at how quickly I got into the girls' sports world as soon as Ella asked about it. Which sport could we angle into? I watched a few games of box lacrosse on TV, so maybe lacrosse goalie looked promising. I passed by my old swimming pool and saw some kid do an inward dive, which brought a "hmmmmm" to my lips. Tennis lessons, that's the ticket. After my wife's friend mentioned her son did fencing in college, and at a really good college at that, I drove by the storefront fencing school in the nearby industrial park and looked at the price of épées.

I started to get a twinge that my girls could be The Ones, the kids who got written up in the papers and maybe played on TV a few times. Oh, it wasn't the same as the dads of boys, I'm sure. Boys, well, they could be on trading cards and have on-camera interviews and play in stadiums filled with drunken alumni. I was never going to confuse the two, I suppose, but I also wasn't going to let any trick I could think of go untried.

For instance, as soon as they were able to hold a bat in tee-ball, which starts in kindergarten, I taught Ella and Sylvia to hit left handed. It was both a long-term and short-term strategy. Most often, a lesser fielder—or perhaps no fielder at all—plays second base in girls' softball, and left-handers usually hit the ball toward second base, so there is a greater chance of a left-handed batter getting a hit. Furthermore, since the left-hand batting box is closer to first base, even slower runners have a jump on beating out a routine ground ball. Ella reveled in her diamond left-handedness, often getting ground-ball home runs, which passed by dandelion-watching second basegirls and right fielders with regularity. Also, being the odd one always gets a kid noticed. This wasn't the kid slicing up spiders in math class or shooting out owls' eyes with a slingshot, just a left-handed batter for coaches to "ooh" over.

It was maniacal, certainly, but so satisfying. More often than not, I stood watching these games with other perplexed, but maybe inwardly as maniacal, dads. Sylvia was on an early soccer team where all but three players were from families of all girls, and all of the rest had first-born girls. It seems like the best girl athletes in town—or at least the ones who started the earliest—were daughters of dads similarly situated, with no boys to pin those drunken-cheering-alumni hopes to. The Kieps, the Brandts, the Ngs, the Lupinskis, the Yakos, the Lennys, the Ciemnys, the Carsons, the Mateers—it spanned ethnic, religious, social, and financial classes, these all-girl or first-girl families. We had girls who were attracted to sports. Or did we dads attract them thus? No one admitted the latter, to be sure. It was too late in the feminist revolution for anyone to own up to that. Our girls were going to be jock grrlz of their own choosing.

I found out early that I was not going to be the coach of any of this. I had two major flaws, at least in the realm of youth coaching. First, I discovered I could never reprimand any but my own kids. As soon as some kid got out of line, I would look for another adult to pull her back in. In the back of my mind were the eyes of the kid's parents, searing through me, ready to pounce on my attempted thwarting of their daughter's creativity.

Worse, though, I was as squeamish as a three-year-old before a measles booster shot at the thought of calculating equal playing time. As any youth coach has to know, playing time is to an overinvolved sports parent as a wife joke was to Henny Youngman: Too much is never enough.

The quest for playing time cannot start too early for some parents. When Ella first played biddie soccer, at maybe five or six, there was a saint of a woman who oversaw the rabble on Haddonfield's rut-filled—and runt-filled—Radnor Field. Biddie soccer is little more than a scrum of courageous kids flailing at the ball with outstretched limbs of all sorts while the deathly afraid swing their legs a good twenty-five feet away in hopes of never coming in contact with a ball or another kid.

In this context, playing time is about as relevant as a Green Party candidate at a presidential debate. Half the kids want to play all the time, and the other half would sooner be watching Lou Dobbs reruns on the tube. Yet one day, as Haddonfield legend has it, the mother of a kindergarten girl of the Dobbsian sentiment marched up to the supervisor, who was trying her best to make sure the purples were on the field with the yellows and the orange kid with his foot stuck in the net wouldn't be angling for ankle surgery. The woman corralled the supervisor and demanded more playing time for her daughter. The daughter, cowering behind her blustering mother, was either sick with embarrassment or already sick of soccer. The supervisor surveyed her universe of scramblers and whimperers; to be sure, at least a few kids actually having fun. She then said the words all overwrought sports parents should hear upon signing their first medical consent form:

"Lady, if you want a scholarship, play the oboe."

I remembered that the day the music teacher was going to install Sylvia as the first-seat clarinet in the Haddonfield

Middle School orchestra. She hid the clarinet in a dusty corner of the music room, from which we finally extricated it about two months later.

"I will never pick up that thing again," said Sylvia, dropping her best skill. I don't think there was a big chance for Benny Goodmanesque quality there, but like most kids in high-pressure sports towns like Haddonfield, Sylvia had clearly made her choice.

The crush of youth sports, at least in modern suburbia, comes almost all at once, between kindergarten and second grade. There is a lot to choose from, but everyone chooses almost everything. No one wants his or her kid to get too far behind in the sporting race. Even if I had wanted to be above that fray, I wouldn't have known how to avoid it. The girls wanted to be with their friends at every possible moment, and whether it was soccer in the fall, basketball in the winter, or softball in the spring, that was the way to do it.

It was all organized, too, and handed down from the previous generation. There were tryout schedules and reserved fields and time slots for each venue. Sylvia or Ella and I might have impromptu catches and throws and kicks and hits in the backyard or on the sidewalk, but it was mostly parent–kid. Rarely did two kids or five kids or a host of kids throw a ball around anywhere. From when they started in sports, from those first kicks in soccer and at bats in tee-ball, the girls met only for practice or games.

It was disconcerting to someone like me, who quit Little League at age nine but played baseball (or some form like Wiffle ball or wire ball or halfball) almost every spring or summer evening. I got tired of the same lament from other, mostly male parents—"When we were kids, we played on our own"—but I had to admit I felt the same way.

Ella and Sylvia didn't seem to lament much. Perhaps it was easier for them, at ages five, six, and seven, to be scheduled for soccer on Mondays and Wednesdays and basketball on whatever nights it was and to know that Christine or Sarah or Sophie would be there. It was much harder for me to get them to practice piano, with its vague half hours somewhere in the week, than to get them to put on their cutesy uniforms and head to the field at those circumscribed times.

Thus, sports became our choice venue of togetherness, if not from convenience then from a mutual desire to cleave to a schedule, something the modern two-worker, suburban, climbing family has a penchant for. Both Sylvia and Ella, from their earliest sporting days in the beginning years of grammar school and despite differing personalities, were amenable to it, too.

Most parents blessed with more than one kid are baffled that two kids in the same house, with the same parents and most of the time eating the same things and wearing the same clothing, can be as different as, say, Aquaman and Bullwinkle J. Moose. Ella and her sister Sylvia, three and a half years younger, are such a pair.

Ella looks like my side of the family, and Sylvia appears to have sprung from my wife as her Mini-Me. Ella learned early on to suck up and sweet talk to get her way. Sylvia just does whatever she wants, and damn the consequences. Ella grew to all of five-feet-zero, so hustling and running everywhere was essential. Sylvia passed her in height by the time she was six and decided that running was an option to be avoided whenever possible.

Each time she looked at a sport, Sylvia found the path of least leg movement. As soon as the position was open, she became the soccer goalie, for instance. She saw the extra arc on the basketball court and asked me what it was for.

"You get three points if you throw it in from there," I said, and then added the line that swayed her: "No need to go any further." She was the first girl of her cadre to develop a three-point shot and rarely ever again drove to the hoop. She became a goalie in lacrosse as well, even though that meant getting pelted by hard rubber balls at close range. It did mean no running.

A few years later, when Sue and I went to Calvin Coolidge's birthplace in Vermont—I am both an inveterate traveler and a presidential trivia nut—we bought a T-shirt with a Coolidge quote on it for Sylvia. It read, "I do not choose to run," Coolidge's response to those who implored him to go for a new term in 1928. Though not yet in her teens at the time we gave it to her, Sylvia got the joke and threw the shirt back at us immediately.

Still, I had to give Sylvia her props. I play a lot of basketball, and the three-point line is about the outside of my range. When she started lofting threes as early as third grade, she shot a bit from the chest but otherwise with good form and a wrist-bent follow-through. Even though she wasn't a starter, her first travel team coach, Tom Betley, developed an in-bound play just for her. He would take the much-faster Emily Carson out of the game for a moment and have Sylvia throw in the ball. The two tallest girls would form a double-pick at the foul line, and Sylvia would lumber around behind them. She'd get the ball back and—kaboom—make her three about 60 percent of the time. The next out-of-bounds time stoppage, Emily would be back in, but Sylvia had her role.

From early on, then, the girls had their after-schools, their weekends, and an earnest amount of time in between filled with the wonder of the field, the diamond, the court, and the pool. I was left to figure out how to be the dad who give sage advice, as I had to Ella after the first Haddon Heights game we saw together, and revel in the idea that girls could not only be beautiful and smart but also hit home runs and swish three-pointers.

The Biddie Sports Quadrangle

Soccer, Swim and Dive, Softball, and Basketball

As the elementary school years moved along, sports became a bigger part of the Strauss girls' schedule. There were enough sports possibilities that by the time they were getting bored with one, a new one came up. There seemed to be four dominant sports: soccer, which took place in the fall and spring; softball, which split with soccer in the spring; basketball, which had seasons in the winter and summer; and swimming and diving, which for us was primarily a summer thing but for other kids was a year-round grind.

Soccer, though, seemed to have taken over Haddonfield, and I was perplexed and annoyed about it. Youth suburban soccer can do a sports dad in, even one predisposed to think well of the sport.

When I was in elementary school, one of our neighbors brought her father over from England to live with the family. His name was Charlie, and, no doubt just looking for some way to pass the time, he became the janitor at Woodcrest School. During after-lunch recess, he would bring out his old, beat-up soccer ball and kick it around. Most of us schoolkids didn't believe people in their fifties or sixties, as I imagine Charlie was back then, would do anything remotely athletic. But Charlie was one of us. School janitors had a respect from us kids that they presumably did not from adults. He worked in school when we did, and lunchtime recess was for him, too.

So on that one day in fifth grade when Charlie finally called a bunch of us over to kick the ball with him, we weren't hesitant in the least. Probably two or three of us had actually heard of soccer—we're talking about 1961 in the United States here—but not one of us had ever actually touched a soccer ball or even seen one up close.

Over what may have only been a few weeks, Charlie did his best to try to teach us boys—as with treehouses and secret handshakes, girls were not allowed into this kind of mid-twentieth-century activity—some dexterity with our feet. I can't imagine he was that successful, as none of us ended up playing soccer in high school. We all went back to patriotic American sports like kickball and running bases and dodgeball and bombardment by the end of fifth grade.

These days, a teacher seen allowing recess dodgeball or bombardment would be strung up by some child protection agency. About twenty years ago, though, someone somewhere decided that Americans could no longer hide from the rest of the world's favorite sport and introduced soccer to his kid's preschool.

Perhaps as much as Jefferson's Declaration, Einstein's *MC* squared, Disney's Mickey, or Ford's assembly line, the indoctrination of toddlers to organized soccer has changed American life. In fact, Ford's assembly line had to be reconfigured to make the vans so valued by soccer moms, who then changed the American landscape by voting first for Bill Clinton and then for George W. Bush, the only two Baby Boomer presidents.

There is nothing inherent in soccer for me to hate. After all, I am an unabashed international. I love seeing oddball countries; I've dragged my kids for lunches in San Marino and Liechtenstein, trips to Colombia and Botswana and El Salvador and Jordan, and a spring vacation in Malta (because it was the only Western European country I had never been to). In all those lands, soccer is beyond gut-wrenching passion, the national sport by far.

Soccer in the United States, particularly in middle- to upper-class suburbs, is merely a way to bring the Ugly American in all of us to the fore. In its rudiments, any toddler, even one with no discernible coordination, can do it. It seems that kids instinctively want to kick the crap out of other kids. At its base, there are no other skills necessary in soccer, so any kid can do it.

Furthermore, since soccer is "European," those four-wheel-drive-wielding strivers from the suburbs need desperately to have their kids buy in. Look, I'm sure Tim Howard, the U.S. national team goalie, is a wonderful guy and a good athlete. But he is a half–African American, half-Hungarian kid from New Jersey with Tourette's syndrome: a Volvo-driving, Starbucks-drinking *New Yorker* reader's dream. If Howard's vitae doesn't scream "Soccer!" what does?

Ella did not embrace soccer early on. Oh, she played in the toddler leagues—I think she was on the team with the purple T-shirts—but when, at age six, the five-day-a-week gotta-practice-soccer mania started, she recoiled.

Soccer's modern suburban foothold seems to stem from what I call the Second-Best Kid syndrome. In basketball, for instance, you actually have to make a basket or two, or perhaps block a shot, to show how decent you are. Softball requires coordination to get a hit. Soccer, who knows? At age six, you kick the ball a couple of times and Mom can squeal ecstatically. During traveling team games, usually the parents on the sidelines will acknowledge who the best girl is, but an overwhelming majority have at least the vague belief that their own daughter is the Second-Best Kid, worthy of a scholarship to a prestigious university or at least a solid Division II program. The devils on those parents' shoulders, dribbling the spotted soccer ball, have sucked them in.

Soccer camps start practically out of the womb in Haddonfield. For a few years, they were hosted by a British twentysomething who called himself Soccer Sam. Sometimes, I thought Sam put on the British accent just to sound more attractive to soccer parents. Soccer has completely taken over a reconstituted dump on the outskirts of town, hard by the train line between Philadelphia and Atlantic City. It is called Crows Woods, and though there are victory garden–type planting areas, several softball fields, and hiking and running trails, there are really only two things people in town think of when you mention Crows Woods: youth soccer and teenage nighttime drinking—and I am not so sure it is fortunately more the first than the latter.

Though the drainage system at Crows Woods is abominable and the winds howl there in early spring and late fall, hundreds of well-heeled—or well-cleated—Haddonfield soccer scions populate it almost constantly. It's hard to argue with the long-term results: The Soccer Sam et al.–trained kids have won South Jersey high school titles and the occasional state championship regularly. High school baseball and softball hardly get a blip in comparison.

But none of this soccer has become recreational. Nothing but clinics and meaningful games seem to get played at Crows Woods. The last time something akin to pickup ever happened was when Ella was in fifth grade. A barely lighted corner field, too small and ill-kept for the real soccerphiles, was left for recreational soccer. It was only Friday nights and was full of misfits that only *Glee*, the TV show about a nerdy high school glee club, could love. There was the fat kid who would kick the ball far and laugh boisterously at the thought of spindly-legged girls chasing it, the attention deficit disorder kid who would run in circles when he wasn't actually near the ball, and the kid with Down syndrome who was pretty much as good as anyone else. Girls played with boys, and fourth graders played with middle schoolers. No one complained, and no one even remembered the score seconds after he or she came off the field, giggling and high-fiving. Parents, oblivious to the tension of the practices of the soccer-gensia around them, used the time to exercise on the walking track or catch up on the week's newspapers.

Of course, when Haddonfield decided to have third-grade travel soccer the next year and usurp the field, recreational Friday night soccer was banned forever. Sports for the fun of it, R.I.P.

Swimming also was a year-round suburban obsession Ella and Sylvia managed to eschew. It's not that they didn't want to swim, but there was something un-finny about them. We belonged to the old swim club where I hung out as a kid, Woodcrest Pool. Ella took swim lessons there every summer starting at age five, having to have at least four lessons each June just to swim the three or four lengths of the pool and earn the colored band that allowed her to go into the pool on her own. In the winter, we would try to keep the stroke going with lessons at the local YMCA; it was like a booster tetanus shot and, to Ella, about as painful.

All these suburban pools had their own summer swim teams. By age eight, if you weren't doing the 50-meter butterfly in something like a half second short of the Olympic record, you were on the brink of amphibious ostracism. Ella came home crying one day fearing that she would never be invited to a pool-party birthday celebration for her lack of swimming prowess. Sylvia was only marginally better, needing only the summer lessons each year. Her more cynical attitude served her well as she dismissed summer swim teams as a cult, as if donning swim team bathing suits in summer caused her friends to grow long facial hair and whiskers and howl at the moon.

Sylvia perversely lit out for the diving team at Woodcrest Pool. Whereas the swimmers had to be at practice somewhere around 7 A.M., and it was interminable, the divers didn't start until 9 or 10 and practiced for only an hour. A slew of kids were both swimmers and divers, but Sylvia was going to be a specialist at age six. Furthermore, swim meets tended to be interminable as well, and there were about eight of them a summer. Dive meets went quickly, and there were only three of them. Not only that, but in diving, your kid is out of the water while doing the trick, so a parent can actually see it. Every kid in a cap and shaved skin doing the Australian crawl looks the same in the pool.

Most of the dives six-year-olds learn are pretty under-standable. In fact, two of the required ones are front jump and back jump, so simple a barely watching parent can get it. The first year, Sylvia didn't get much past those. There was a front dive and then, for the last three weeks or so, there was an attempt at a back dive, which almost always ended up being a back jump. The coach, a peppy kid who was on the University of Wisconsin swim team, would stand on the board and hold Sylvia in a back bend at least a dozen times during each practice. This was patience enough for sainthood many times over, but I don't think it resulted in more than three or four actual back dives.

Ella, feeling a bit challenged by her younger sister trying this minor bit of acrobatics, decided to attempt diving when she was about eleven, still young enough to catch on. By that time, Sylvia had gone on from the back dive to an inward, which means the diver faces the board but dives forward, requiring a jump back so her head doesn't hit the board on the way down. This was scary enough for Ella, but it really freaked out my wife, Sue. The first time she saw Sylvia doing it at a pool party, she almost ran for cover and made certain I had my medical card on me whenever I was at diving practice.

One of the diving meets that year was at Wedgewood, the fancier club in Haddonfield where most of Ella's friends belonged. About a dozen of those friends were on both the swim and dive teams, so when Woodcrest, a plebeian pool in nearby tract-house Cherry Hill, and the teams from even lesser towns, came we looked a bit shoddy in comparison. Still, the Wedgewood girls greeted Ella and Sylvia with warmth, and the competition began.

The Wedgewood girls did all the requisite dives—and some of the more intricate ones with twists and flips—pretty well. Ella was still on front jump, back jump, and regular old dive routine, with one or two other no-frill dives.

When the scores were announced at the end of the meet, Ella was thirty-sixth in her age group, which was dead last. She managed a weak smile over to her Wedgewood girlfriends and then a somber frown about a foot deep on each end as she trudged over to me.

Time for a life lesson.

I went into what must have been an overbearingly long diatribe for an eleven-year-old whose spirit undoubtedly had been crushed. I told her she had actually done every dive, which was more than a few kids who had been disqualified, so thirty-sixth wasn't really last, last, last. I told her of the honor one kid each year got at Carleton College, my alma mater. It was for the student who actually graduated but had the lowest grade point average of anyone who did. It was a fine line, to be sure, but that kid who may have teetered over it landed on the right side, which took a whole lot of fortitude. This teetering but coming out whole, I told her, was what she had just done.

I told her it was only about noon on a beautiful day, and we were at her friends' pool, so why not have fun. The frown stayed down, but she did trudge back to the pack of Wedgewoodians. For a moment, they gasped together, but then they broke out in a big round of applause and chanted, "El-la, El-la, El-la!" She looked back at me, still a bit dubious, and I gave her the A-okay hand signal.

Ella never dove competitively again, but I still remind her that it was probably my favorite moment for her in sports.

I never warmed to soccer or swimming, and I was all too happy when the girls wanted to play softball or basketball. I was never good at baseball, but the Phillies had been my first favorite team, so I always had a spectator's interest in it. The Woodcrest Little League field was only a few blocks from my house, and as a preteen I was over there at least three times a week in season to see my first local heroes play and get a nightly cherry sno-cone.

I was pretty miserable at baseball, to tell the truth. When Little League started, about age eight, I was in my chubby period and therefore relegated to catcher, the least glamorous position for younger kids, no matter how wonderful Yogi Berra or Roy Campanella were. It was also one where embarrassment and injury were rife. I opted out at age nine and stuck with the sno-cones thereafter.

But I became the idiot savant of baseball trivia—the Sultan of Stats, if you will—of the schoolyard. These days, computers keep every last bit of arcana for the fantasy league milieu. Back in the mid-twentieth century, though, I was the one consulted during every argument or after every trade because I actually knew all the third-string catchers in the league and their statistics, meaningful and bizarre. I admit, I would have rather been like my Woodcrest friends Jack Deeney, who had a shockingly good curveball at age ten, and Mike Stein, whom we nicknamed "Spit" because that's what he did, shaking his head while running like the proverbial wind. Yet we do what we can, and for me that was knowing about J. Owen Wilson, the otherwise mediocre player who amassed thirty-six triples in 1912, something not even closely approached since, or John Boozer, a relative failure as a Phillies relief pitcher who was known for spitting tobacco on the ceiling of the clubhouse and catching it, open-mouthed, as it dripped back downward.

So when it came time to analyze what would help my kids advance in sports, I naturally took the oddball edge. Ella had no sooner started out in tee-ball than I was at the ready. Tee-ball was the perfect five-year-old sport for such a Quaker-but-intense town as Haddonfield. Every kid gets an at bat in tee-ball, no matter how many outs have been made. Still, parents tense up when their kid is at the tee. If their kid is the one who barely skims the ball with the bat or, heaven forfend, actually blows right by and misses it, the parents feel the shame of the misbegotten. A blast that goes into the outfield sends the parental cheer into a third octave.

Ella and later Sylvia were in the vast middle at tee-ball, happy just to hit the ball and circle the bases one by one as each of their friends got their vast-middle singles as well. The merry march around the bases occurred about twice a week in the spring, but around the second week, I decided that Ella needed a leg up. I told her to go to the other side of the tee and hit left-handed. As with most of my suggestions—and this hasn't changed since she entered young adulthood—she gave me a slight crooked grimace, then shrugged her shoulders, then gave it a shot. She still got her tee-ball single each time, but the die was cast. Coach-to-be fathers gave her a second look. To a biddie softball coach, left-handedness is a valued commodity, as it is in the major leagues. I had laid the groundwork for future stardom.

Tee-ball was a nonsexist activity, at least on the surface. Boys and girls played together, which seemed to please them. But you could see that the dads of boys were getting haughty already. I would get condescending tones from them when Ella or Sylvia got a shot off the tee, knowing that soon my girls would be relegated to the world of softball while the other parents would be watching Johnny or Mikey on the vaunted Haddonfield Little League fields.

The girls seemed oblivious to this and often asked me to play catch or throw a Wiffle ball to them in the backyard. I don't think they were trying to improve; it was just that baseball was the game to be played as the weather got better outside and a way to have Dad as a playmate when none their age was available. The bat-and-ball games were not a passion but a pastime.

Basketball was my passion, and in those early years the girls caught that passion and claimed it, too. When I reflect on how many basketball games I have played, the places I have played them, and the characters with whom I have played, I have to ask myself, "How come I never became any good?" I have played pickup games in Gaza and in Ouagadougou, the capital of the poverty-stricken West African country of Burkina Faso. Real, live NBA players, however mistakenly, have guarded me, and every once in a while, I have hit a three-pointer to win a game.

In my fifties, I manage to play about five times a week in various venues around Philadelphia and South Jersey. Most often, I can find someone to guard, but most often, too, I am the worst player on the court.

I'm betting my father was of the same ilk. On the other hand, his best friend at Temple University was a guy named Ike Richman. Ike became, as they say, a *macher*, a mover and shaker and a lawyer of some repute in Philadelphia. One of his clients in the early 1960s was the best basketball player of the era (and probably ever, *pace* Michael Jordan), Wilt Chamberlain. Another of his clients was Irv Kosloff, a manufacturer of paper products, whom Ike helped to buy the Syracuse Nationals of the National Basketball Association in 1963 and move them to Philadelphia as the 76ers. For that legal help, Ike got a piece of the team. A year later—no surprise—the 76ers, in a lopsided trade, got Wilt from the San Francisco Warriors.

What that meant for me is that Ike gave my father four decent Sixers tickets a couple of times a year, which meant that I got to impress my basketball-loving friends. It also got my mother to meet a fellow West Philadelphian. My mom grew up at 52nd and Chestnut streets, and Wilt was from a few blocks farther west.

Anyway, one night when I was in high school, my parents were invited to a Bonds for Israel dinner for Ike. The idea of these dinners was that American Jews would come to a dinner for some famous person and buy a bond that would support the still-fledgling nation of Israel. Ike must have been fairly famous. The co-chairs of the event were Philadelphia mayor James H. J. Tate and comedian Joey Bishop, part of the Sinatra Rat Pack and, despite his Catholic-sounding stage name, a Jewish Philadelphian. Also at the dinner were various Philly politicos and sports types and a young comic named Bill Cosby.

When my parents came home, my mom couldn't wait to tell me her news.

"I sat with that Wilt Chamberlain, Robert, and you couldn't believe how tall he was," she said to me, I much more breathless than she at the sublime revelation. "He got up when he met me and he just went up, and up, and up, Robert. And he was wearing a yarmulke."

Then she presented me with what is still my most precious bit of memorabilia. It was the program from the dinner—Mayor Tate's and Joey Bishop's and Bill Cosby's names inside—with a multicolored artistic rendering of the Hebrew alphabet on the cover. To the right of the first letter (Hebrew is read right to left), the aleph is the signature of the 76ers all-star forward, Chet Walker, and over a few more letters to the left of that is the sacred scrawl of Chamberlain. Inherently, it is worth little, because Walker and Chamberlain signed thousands of things over the years, but when I look at it I can only think of Mom and her handshake with Wilt as he went "up, and up, and up."

Sadly, both my parents were dead by the time Ella and Sylvia were born, but I am sure they would have been there when I first took each of them to the Haddon Heights Summer Basketball Camp. Kenny Hamburger ran his camp in the Haddon Heights High School gym, in which he was a star. He was only about 6 feet tall, but in high school he was the shooter, the passer, the captain in a family of athletes in a town even smaller than Haddonfield. He tore up his knee soon after high school, but he did not lose his ardor for the game.

Kenny employed high school players and coaches from the area to help little ones like Ella and Sylvia learn the basics and, above all, have fun. There were shooting and dribbling games and jumps around hula hoops and lots of contests and prizes. Kenny and his instructors knew basketball, but, Kenny having been a preschool and elementary teacher, they knew even better how to get every kid to smile. Sadly, camps like his have vanished and hard-assed drill sergeant camps have taken their place. I don't know, maybe my girls would have been in the WNBA by now if they had had to do twenty-five pushups every time they missed a foul shot at age seven, but the many photos I have of those "Kenny Camps," as we called them, show only smiling kids, many of whom became high school standouts.

The winter after the first few weeks of Kenny Camp, Ella was anxious to join her first Haddonfield recreation team. The coach was Rich Edwards, a television news executive who barely had a minute of spare time but was willing to coach when no one else, including me, stepped up. Similarly, when before the first game he asked who wanted to bring the ball up, no one volunteered except Ella, so Rich gave her the nod.

The first time up the court, Ella dribbled as Kenny had shown her, with her body tilted forward and her head up. The other nine girls, perhaps dazed, came nowhere near her, so she just dribbled to the basket, which was about 6 feet high, rather than the normal 10, and lofted in a layup.

The girl from the other team attempted to dribble upcourt next, but as Kenny had instructed her, Ella deftly slapped the ball just to her left at about midcourt and dribbled forward through the morass of girls, all waving their arms and splaying their legs. Ella was not at all rattled and just progressed forward, again making a nearly uncontested layup.

The other team then passed the ball a few times, which was quite impressive, but eventually Ella had had enough of that and grabbed the ball from one of the girls. Unconcerned that there were other girls all around her, she dribbled slowly up the court again and threw in another layup.

How proud was I? The score was Ella, 6; everyone else in Haddonfield's second grade, zip. The scholarship was practically within our grasp.

Then Rich Edwards called time-out. He gathered the girls around him, and I could see him look first at Ella. I tiptoed to within earshot and got my comeuppance.

"You know, Ella," Rich said, rather sternly, "there are other girls on the team. You could think about passing to them."

I tiptoed, rather more quickly, back to my corner. Ella nodded and apologized. I don't think she scored the rest of the game, but she threw pass after pass to the right girls, whether they could catch them or not, just as, apparently, Kenny had taught her.

First game, first lesson learned. Rich set her on the right path, one from which, I hoped, she would never veer.

"Daddy, that was fun," she said after the game. "Mr. Edwards is the best. Fun. Fun. Fun. Fun."

She did a spin in the air and shot an imaginary layup. Jock-daughter-induced tears welled up in my eyes for the first, and certainly not the last, time. The sparkle was in Ella's eyes, as it would be for Sylvia in those single-digit years, but somehow, just about when nine turns to ten in the modern youth sports world, something changes—maybe more for parents than kids, but even for them. I don't know that the sparkle loses its shimmer, but the transition to seriousness starts. Maybe, like in the Disney version of *Peter Pan*, Tinker Bell flickers in and out a little bit. It was going to be good that Ella and Sylvia got more proficient, but those days of no-worry spins in the air would be a little harder to come by.

Getting Serious

In 1999, when the girls were seven and four, respectively, we moved across town to a bigger house with a long driveway that ended at a pre-automobile barn/garage that all the owners before us had kept lovingly authentic. A still-sweet-smelling wood-frame building, it had two old horse stalls with sliding wooden doors between them. The trapdoor from the loft to the manger still flipped up, ready for the feed to slide down. There was a split "Mr. Ed" door separating the old horse area from the garage. Mr. Ed, as early-baby-boom parents will remember, was a horse who spoke English, but only to his master, Wilbur. Wilbur would amble—or maybe trudge—out to the barn/garage to commiserate with Mr. Ed when things, mostly just domestic 1960s sitcom spats, weren't going well inside the house.

I did not envision getting a talking horse to console me in my dotage, perhaps because one of the first things I did when we bought the house was asphalt over the end of the cracked concrete driveway and have a good fiberglass backboard cemented in, the better for the girls and me to take our casual frustrations out on a few 15-footers with, perhaps, a capping reverse layup.

That wasn't all, though. Out behind the barn was a 1-acre field with a worn-down metal sign attached to the entrance from the back of our driveway reading "Marion Wood Nature Sanctuary." It was filled with a dozen or more species of trees and bushes and a big open space of grassland at its center. Our new house, a seven-bedroom Victorian with ornate gingerbread trimmings, faced onto a busy street, and there were houses all along the four sides of the block in which the Marion Wood acre was encased. No one going too fast for the neighborhood on West End Avenue would have imagined that well-sculpted acre behind the barn. A century before, it was attached to our property, even though our house was hardly the biggest, the oldest, or the most distinctive on the four streets that surrounded it.

I took this as a sign that no matter what its formal name, the acre of grass and woodlands should be the new Strauss Athletic Complex (A.C.). When I was a boy, a former Long Island University basketball coach, Clair Bee, had written a series of adolescent sports novels starring a Frank Merriwell–like character, Chip Hilton. Chip's father, Big Chip, died before the Little Chip got to high school, which is where the novels begin. Before his demise, Big Chip had outfitted the backyard into the Hilton A.C., primarily for the major sports, football, basketball, and baseball, with hoops, mounds, goalposts, and the like. Chip and his friends were out there constantly, and the widow Mrs. Hilton did a lot of sighing and smiling, looking out the kitchen window at them, while always baking something marvelous for the boys.

Furthermore, Chip's friends were a diverse lot, more appropriate to the politically correct current age than to the Eisenhower-dry 1950s. There was an Irish kid, a Hispanic kid, a black kid, and, almost ready-made for me, the Jewish galoof, Biggie Cohen.

Chip was the star of every team, even when he wasn't. He broke his leg, but he didn't let his team down and became the basketball manager. He bunted his runner friends over in crucial situations, when he could have gone for glory and tried for a home run. He always complimented his teammates to reporters. He loved his mom.

The Strauss A.C. would be the same for my Golden Girls. My first buy was a pitchback, one of those springy-netted things that they could kick or throw their balls into incessantly, even when alone. Sylvia wanted to learn archery, so we bought a Styrofoam cube with a target on its face. Though there was no room for a real diamond, there were plenty of well-spaced trees for Wiffle ball and a big planting of bamboo by the fence for home run territory.

Of course, the sacred ground would be the hoop, a few yards north of the Marion Wood. It was just far enough from Mom's garden to leave room for a high school three-pointer, and the garage doors were at the right angle to push off for a good layup drill. I didn't really teach the girls much, just hung out and rebounded when necessary. In time, I didn't even have to let them beat me in shooting games like H-O-R-S-E or 21. They did quite well on their own.

Sylvia was always the more serious about shooting. At age ten, she was on a summer squad formed by a woman who coached the high school team in a nearby town. Mrs. O'Neill expected the girls to try one hundred shots of various kinds at least four times a week. Sylvia, like me, was a quirky obsessive. In this case, she wrote down the results on a blackboard and did her best to beat them the next day. The goal wasn't getting any better stylistically, just having a higher score. Sometimes, I caught her examining the blackboard later on.

"Seventeen, a really good number. Way better than 16," I heard her mutter one day. "Way better," as if the shape of the regal seven were more glorious than a pudgy-bottomed six.

About the same time as she was recording left-handed layups and the like, she started playing with an old set of 3-inch-high white figurines of the presidents of the United States my dad had bought for me and I had stored in an old wooden cigar box. Given my age, the figurines went up only to Lyndon Johnson, but that did not faze Sylvia. One day, I saw a lineup of seven of the guys on Sylvia's nightstand, with William Howard Taft a few inches ahead of the others.

"What's with Taft?" I asked her.

"It's Friday," she answered, as if I were a moron.

"So, what's that got to do with it?" I retorted, only slightly moronically.

"It's Friday, so Taft is ahead," she said, and left the room.

It was not the last time Sylvia made me feel as if I were in a Samuel Beckett play.

There is a well-watched clip of a toddler Tiger Woods making some golf shots on *The Mike Douglas Show,* a syndicated variety talk TV show of the 1970s and 1980s, taped in the Philadelphia studios of KYW-TV, where I would later work. In retrospect, it is the nascency of parental overbearingness in youth sports. Oh, it's not that parents didn't shove footballs into their kids' hands in the crib before that, but this Tiger thing was on TV, and the kid really did end up amounting to something.

Like I said, I used to work in TV and can attest to the tube's mystical powers. I periodically brought friends to the news shows I produced and let them sit by the news sets to see the broadcast live. Invariably, they still watched the show on the monitors, as if the anchors' actual bodies were less real than their images on the screen. Furthermore, since I was the producer in the control room, often in a frenzy during the broadcast, on three phones and with a dozen screens in front of me, most of my friends decided that this was the most alluring thing they had ever seen.

"This is a real chick magnet," or something like it, was the idea. It was dark and dank in that control room, but somehow my friends thought it sexy. It was particularly annoying to me when some goof on one of the dozen screens in front of me waved his arms behind a reporter during a live shot. To him, and apparently to my friends, being on TV, no matter how inconsequentially, was the verification of life itself.

So it is no wonder that barely any of Ella's or Sylvia's first games were seen live by many parents; nearly all those parents were at the fields fumbling with their new video cameras, maybe not quite channeling their kids' inner Tiger but at least having a record just in case it emerged.

Fortunately, despite my stint in producing TV news, I was a Luddite when it came to video cameras. After failing to capture Ella's first words, first steps, or even a good tantrum, I gave up the suburban Fellini in me. I didn't want to lug the soccer chair—regardless of the sport, they were always called "soccer" chairs, to my chagrin—from the car, so why would I want to carry something else, something I couldn't figure out how to use anyway?

I have to admit I am sorry I don't have some video of Ella in softball, though. She looked incongruously cute in her cap, which never fit her right. I think it is because she didn't always have a ponytail, which the other girls slipped through the hole in the back, over the size-adjusting strap. Ella's cap tenuously balanced on her bowl-cut, ready to fly windward like that of Willie Mays rounding second on the way to a triple.

The cap did come off a lot in those early years. Hitting left-handed as she did, she was both closer to first base—which isn't far away in seven-year-old softball—and hitting into the teeth of the weed-watching second basegirls and right-fielders. I've always believed that what most people think of as hitting left-handed is actually inverted. The control in batting is with the arm facing the pitcher: It has the power and is the last one holding the bat on a swing. Thus, if you are in the "left-handed" batting box, the one closest to first base, you are really controlling the bat with your right hand, and that is where natural right-handers should be.

So Ella, and later Sylvia, took naturally to the "left-handed" role at bat. Since dads put the best fielders at shortstop, third base, and left field, where "right-handed" hits most often ended up, Ella and Sylvia were set up to always hit to the lesser fielders. Since she was also speedy, Ella hit many a ground ball home run past those right-side fielding girls, who probably would rather have been ripping out their fingernails with rusty tweezers than be out there in their geeky softball uniforms.

After a few games, Ella inserted herself at second base in the field, perhaps because she saw so many of her own hits slice through that position. She evidently had the idea that she was responsible for everything the other team hit. She would range far right to grab balls away from the pitcher and shortstop. And she would get terribly impatient with any first basegirl who dropped throws. When catching a grounder at second, she would just run it over to the first base bag to beat out the runner.

My friend Dick, who had noticed the same trait in his athletic and impatient daughter years before, told me, "It's the old 4-U," a good double entendre since "4-U" in baseball-scoring parlance means that the second baseman (designated #4 of the nine fielders by Henry Chadwick, the inventor of baseball scoring) made the putout, unassisted. "She did it, Strauss, for you."

It is hard to imagine the chasm that separates twenty-first-century girls' sports from the sports scene of their fathers unless you look at it through the prism, hazy as it is now, of those fathers' youth. I look at my experience not as unique, though it had some unusual aspects, but as representative and instructional for dads of girl jocks today.

I was an only child and had no one else to play with, fight with, buddy with, or resent. The 1950s were an especially good time for an only boy child to have this kind of sports fantasy life. Families were generally intact, so there were fewer only children than in later times, and there were fewer single-child events, even formal playdates, for doting parents to shuttle us to, thus leaving us more to our own inventions. Ella and Sylvia and their cohorts had schedules parents made for their sports. I had to trust my imagination.

It was also a burgeoning era for big-time sports. Even before the expansion of baseball's major leagues in 1961, clubs in two-team cities were moving to new places. In 1950, there were at least two teams in Philadelphia, Boston, St. Louis, and New York, but each lost at least one team to other locales by 1958. The National Basketball Association, founded in the late 1940s, started becoming more popular by mid-decade, and pro football's "Greatest Game," the 1958 National Football League title game between the Baltimore Colts and New York Giants, made that sport's bones. Newspaper sports sections grew, and radio and television broadcasts became ubiquitous.

It was a real boy thing, though. A girl reading the sports pages or going to a ball game with Dad, much less playing Little League, would have been unheard of in my liberal Republican neighborhood. Historian Doris Kearns Goodwin has written lots about how she bonded with her dad over baseball, but that she got a book out of it proves the contrary point; hers was an anomaly. When I was about ten, my father invited Barbara Sarshik, the daughter of a friend of his, who was also the man who built our house, to a Rutgers football game with us, for what reason I can hardly guess. Barbara and I always got along, but my head grew numb by the second quarter trying to explain to her what was going on in the field. My father must have thought it was cute. When we got home, I pleaded mercy, perhaps even saying I would mow the lawn for the next forty years instead or maybe poke my eyeballs out with a dull stick if I had to go to a game with a girl again.

From the time I could read, I devoured the sports section daily. In summers, I would fiddle with the radio dial, not just listening to easy-to-get Phillies games but tuning in the big-wattage stations in New York and Baltimore, just up the road, or, when ambitious, the ones half a country away, like KMOX in St. Louis for the Cardinals and WHO in Des Moines for the Cubs.

My parents started buying me the boxed "authentic" games. There was an outfit called Avalon Hill in Baltimore that specialized in strategic games, mostly battlefield oriented, but I shunned "Gettysburg" for the baseball game. Most boys of my era remember a football game with a metal "field." There were plastic linemen and backs on little plastic risers. You lined them all up and stuck a small cotton ball in the crook of one back's arm, then turned on a switch. The field vibrated, and all the players buzzed around, practically willy-nilly, until one touched—"tackled"— the ball carrier. I don't know anyone who had the patience to do more than five or six plays on this contraption, but everyone seemed to have one.

The games I played in the rec room, though, were my defining moments. The aforementioned Mr. Sarshik used the bottom floor of his split levels—our model was the "Yale," as opposed to the fancier "Harvard"—for utility rooms, a powder room, and a rudimentary basement, the rec room, with tile floors, a large back window, and rudimentary walls. Early on, I discovered that there were just enough tiles along the length of the room to have each one represent five yards on a football field, with some end zone space.

I would throw the ball to myself, announcing the name of, say, Eagles quarterback Norm Van Brocklin, throwing it to diminutive end Tommy McDonald. As McDonald, I would catch the ball and be tackled (i.e., fall down dramatically) a certain number of tiles away.

In the winter, I would set up my parents' beat-up orange and pink Naugahyde stuffed chair and throw basketballs at it, as the basket. Not only would I announce these games, but I would actually keep score. The major Philadelphia colleges—Temple, Penn, St. Joseph's, Villanova, and La Salle—formed a loose basketball association called The Big Five, and I knew every player. In fact, down in that rec room, I would actually *be* every player, complete with his shooting or passing motions.

Mr. Sarshik had built that rec room, and I had come.

Perhaps because I was always able to imitate the styles of real-life players in my youthful fantasy athletic career, when my kids became old enough, I thought I could be a good team coach. I could not have been more off base.

When Ella and Sylvia got to the point of serious competition, late elementary and middle school years, the call went out for coaches. Knowing that I was somewhat of a jock myself, however lame, most other parents thought I would be coach material, but I just never made the grade.

First of all, I was a devout egalitarian when it came to the all-important issue of playing time. In fact, there is no more important issue in youth sports than playing time. Wars and great political moments have been decided by the apportionment of playing time. For instance, the British generals at the Battle of Trenton gave entirely too much playing time to the second-team Hessians, those German mercenaries, and the underdog Colonials were able to pull off an upset victory, changing the standings of the Revolutionary War League for good. Later on, Coach Washington probably upset the Moms from places like Delaware and Rhode Island but gave the bulk of the playing time to Ben Franklin, Long Tom Jefferson, and Cynical John Adams for the Declaration of Independence. If he'd let Delaware's hero horseman Caesar Rodney, a second-rate Paul Revere, be in there too long, we would still be eating bangers and mash, not to mention steak and kidney pie, rather than succulent cheesesteaks at the Jersey Shore.

Boys, probably even Caesar Rodney, can live without even playing time, especially when they can win the Battle of Trenton. Girls, especially parents of girls, not so much. And I became that side's advocate in the early years.

My greatest achievement as a coach happened on the truncated basketball court at Haddonfield's ancient Central School in one of Sylvia's first town games at about age eight, just before her serious years. Fortunately, the magic number of girls, ten, had shown up for the game. This gave me the opportunity to have them line up and alternatively say, "One" or "Two." The "ones" would play exactly one half the time, and the "twos" would play the other half. Couldn't have been simpler or more Quaker. Lizzie Haddon, in her bloomers, mouth guard, and kneepads, no doubt would have approved.

It worked like a charm, with parents and children all in accord, while the other coach, with eight or twelve kids and no slide rule to figure out equality on the court, was probably getting yelled at by all.

Then, with about four minutes left in the game, I realized that all the girls but the quiet one with the chunky glasses had scored a basket. I called time-out and suspended the equal-playing-time rule. I gathered the girls around and asked them to please pass the chunky-glasses girl the ball and stand in front of her so no one could touch her. Then, she could shoot and score her basket. I crossed my fingers and scrunched up my eyes, waiting for a negative response, but none came. Everyone did the mandatory "Let's Go, Bulldawgs" cheer out of the huddle and, sure enough, the passes and the blockade wall went up summarily.

Unfortunately, the nonscoring girl continued to be a nonscoring girl. Rebound after rebound came our girls' way, and each time, they gathered back into their retaining wall, hiking it back to the shooter. Six or eight shots later, the whistle blew and time was up.

It was my last game as a full-time coach, and I still have the team photo on a bookshelf near me as I type. I volunteered to coach again the next year, but by that age, I had outlived my usefulness. The girls had become more rambunctious, and some had decided they were too good for the others. I found after one practice that I was not good at telling anyone but my own kids what to do, possibly for fear of what their parents would say.

I found myself a new position, though. The harried coaches could never seem to remember what gym practices were in or what times games were. They would routinely give out number 3 (that of local favorite Allen Iverson) too randomly and often hand out uniform number 50—an extra large—to the shortest kid on the team.

This was the stuff those rec room days had prepared me for. I couldn't coach and in some sports I could barely play, but what I could do was be roadie/general manager/press agent/ e-mail guy. As the years went by, I was a whirlwind, negotiating for schedule changes so coaches could go to bar mitzvahs and the like, making sure the snack list was up to date, keeping the scorebook, remembering which girl liked which number, having at least three sets of directions to every venue in parents' e-mails, and knowing how every clock worked in every gym for three counties around.

I started signing every e-mail with my lowercase initials, and even the girls started calling me "rss." Parents decided to enjoy the games, and so few knew how to work a clock that I often had both clock and scorebook duties. In basketball, I had a system that enabled me to track about a dozen different types of stats, from minutiae about turnovers to placement of jump shots. Hey, it passed the time. My daughters at some point ceased to be embarrassed about this and decided that they would at least be able to find a ride to and from games if I were involved.

At the end of every season, I got a gift of some sophisticated wine. Did that mean the parents thought I needed some cooling out on the porch, tipsy time away from being "rss"? Well, maybe, but at least I knew everyone's home and away turnover-to-assist ratio.

As it turned out, it was probably best I couldn't coach, because the girls sincerely wanted to get better in their sports in those late preteen years. Even if their coaches weren't any more versed in the sports than I was, the girls listened to what they had to say and may well have done the eye-rolling thing and ignored me if I were coaching.

It also helped our sporting relationships. Whenever they had a complaint about a teammate or a little thing they wanted to work on, they felt comfortable coming to me for a quick pick-me-up or amble in the Strauss A.C. We could have a five-minute discussion of the game or practice on the ride home, and that was a pleasant transition, not a two-hour lumbering practice with me as a dictator.

Those middle years brought us together in sports, even as they started to become fraught with the supposed need to be "better" for the inevitable tracking that has crept into sports all too soon.

For instance, after a year of tee-ball and another of parent-pitch softball, Sylvia had had it with the dullness of her female teammates barely being able to swing a bat and certainly not being able to handle a swift ground ball.

"I'm playing Little League with the boys this year, and you aren't going to stop me," she told Sue and me in her usual defiant manner.

She got her friend Taylor Ng, the best athlete in her grade, to go to tryouts with her, and coaches Kathleen and Tom Gosse right off the bat and sight unseen took both of them, the only girls to sign up in their age group, for their team. Taylor and Sylvia looked marvelous in the orange uniforms and hats and were as confident as they could be in their eight-year-old-girl triumph. They even did a duet of the consummate baseball song "Centerfield" in the grade school talent show.

Sylvia started the season on a high. Little League, at least on the young end, was no better at coping with left-handed hitters than softball, so she regularly got on base. Taylor was a wunderkind, hitting line drives with precision and verve.

Unfortunately, though, it seemed as if the boys' growth and learning curve hit a rocket upward that spring. As the season wore on, the ground balls Sylvia was beating out came with crisper throws and catches. The balls hit to her became more solid and sharp. Her average fell, and her position in the field moved to the easier spots: right field and, sometimes, catcher.

It may not have helped that Taylor was the best player on the team—in fact, in the whole league.

When it came time to sign up for some kind of ball the next winter, Sylvia was in the netherworld: too good for parent-pitch softball and not quite good enough to be in Little League. Or at least to be a girl in Little League, which meant, as with most glass-ceiling stuff, that the girls had to be twice as good to get half the respect. Even with parents, maybe especially with parents, you didn't want to look unnecessarily pushy, or too feminist, to have a daughter play in upper-level Little League.

She pleaded to go back to Little League, but we pleaded back that she could be the best among the softball players after her season with the boys. Only it would not be so. The softball league started letting girls pitch, which meant nothing went over the plate on a regular basis and almost everything became a walk, a strikeout, or some flailing hit. There was no joy for Sylvia in actually knowing how to play; softball was not going to work out this year or any other year. Taylor stayed in Little League and continued to be the best player in the league until she was twelve or thirteen.

Sylvia felt forced to go to the Dark Side, the world of spring soccer and all that it portended, most prominently the dreaded tryout system and the separation, almost Gulag-like, of the A from the B. It is the defining transition in youth sports, probably similar to what English schoolkids go through with the tests that send one group to university and another to the working class. When his daughter was entering middle school, an old schoolmate told me he wanted to write a book called *Fifth Grade: The Last Innocent Year.* It couldn't be more true in the youth sports world.

From A to B and Back Again
The Agony of the Too-Soon Tryout

The Crows Woods fields, rambling grasslands covering what was, during the years surrounding World War II, the back-edge, almost-out-of-town landfill for our small upscale burg of Haddonfield, were filled with kids wearing pinned-on pieces of paper with numbers and scanner codes emblazoned on them. The week before, Eric Weinrich was jostling and pounding and poking his stick at a bunch of massive men in the Stanley Cup playoffs as a defenseman for the Philadelphia Flyers, who soon after were eliminated in the Cup semifinals. But the event before him seemed to concern him a lot more.

Weinrich stood alone, leaning on a pole that held up the awning roof of the Crows Woods snack bar, looking furtively a couple of fields down. It is not that, despite his celebrity, he felt himself above anyone else there; in fact, it may have been just the opposite, him feeling a bit tentative. His young daughter was trying out for the Haddonfield U-9 travel soccer team. It was May, and the soccer season would not begin until September, when Weinrich, trade bait at the time, might be playing in Chicago or Dallas or Vancouver, not nearby Philadelphia. The

Flyers trained in a rink in Voorhees, two towns over, and like many Flyer families over the years with school-aged children, the Weinriches chose to live in Haddonfield because of the nurturing small school system, and the family ended up staying a few years.

Today, though, what was going on at Crows Woods, not the Forum in Montreal or Madison Square Garden, was what was important.

"Oooh, was that a goal?" Weinrich's twists and turns seemed to ask as he peered out into the distance. "Uhhh, no, just an offsides. Where's the help? Left-foot it. Baby, you can do it. C'mon, the A team is in the balance."

Even to a fifteen-year National Hockey League veteran like Weinrich, his daughter's preteen soccer tryouts were a cause worth biting his nails and using a hodload of body language over. Someone put the broadcast of the Stanley Cup on the snack bar radio, presumably to placate him, but soon after they did, Weinrich ambled as close to the tryout field as he was allowed. Parents are asked to stay back, but he was now far out of earshot of any NHL happening and at least within binocular sight of his daughter's foot flailing.

There is an old saw that says, "You can't live through your kids." I—and no doubt Weinrich, too—would retort, "Then why did you have them?" I could see Weinrich's pain because my daughter, Sylvia, though a little older and on an adjacent field, was trying out for a travel soccer team as well, and I could barely bear to watch, for unlike Weinrich, who was new to the tryout game, I had been there with Ella for several years already. Sylvia was successful this time around in her A quest, but it is a system with thorns and pricks, misplaced joy, and paranoia.

Somewhere around the time of Sylvia's soccer tryout, I drove the carpool back from Hebrew School at the synagogue.

Sylvia attended on a different night, but Ella was there with two classmates and a slightly younger brother of one of them. They were all singing and theater kids, so I thought that for just twenty minutes home I would hear pleasant and noncompetitive talk about *Fiddler on the Roof* or some a cappella fiesta. Long ago, someone told me to always drive the carpool and never say a word. That way, I could learn all the gossip, and the kids would never know where it came from, even though it came directly from them.

"My brother is much more talented than him," said one of the boys, talking about his older sibling, then a junior in high school, and in a rather agitated tone, too. "He should have gotten the part. It's just not fair."

The girl then turned to Ella and said, in almost the same agitated tone, "Yes, and you know, he always wants me to be an alto. I am a soprano and he wants me to be an alto. Unughh."

I had to think Ella was having the same thoughts as I: same garbage, different Dumpster. The older brother and the unsatisfied alto had been relegated to the B team, albeit seemingly a little more personally than in sports.

Despite the theater hierarchy, I still firmly believe that the stigma of the B team in modern suburban sports, maybe even more so in girls' than in boys' sports, is a taint almost too wretched to overcome.

One day in the spring of Ella's fifth-grade year, the dad of one of her friends showed up at our front door unannounced. I suspected something of the worst: secretive drinking, girl backbiting, shoplifting, or cheating in school. Little did I know that it was even worse than that. It was the Grim Reaper of the B team about to cross our threshold.

This dad did not have a long beard, a robe, and a 6-foot scythe like in the *New Yorker* cartoons, but he came with an askew "U.S. Soccer" cap and a few waivers and permission forms. He said the fifth-grade B spring soccer team was short a player or two, and he knew Ella from basketball and thus considered her a pretty good athlete. Would she mind coming on midseason to the team? He even invoked words that the Sirens might have been successful tempting Odysseus with: "I am sure playing time will not be an issue."

It took several weeks for the forms to go through. Youth soccer in twenty-first-century America is a force not to be trifled with. In England, I am guessing, when someone comes to the doorstep and asks whether your kid wants to play on a team, you assent, and then they tell her to show up the next night with her kicking feet in fettle. In the Colonies, though, things are mightily different.

All Ella needed was for me to sign about six waivers, medical forms, and player profiles. She needed a note from her doctor, a current photo for her local league I.D., and another for her U.S. Soccer registration. I needed to give the supplicant dad two copies of her birth certificate and at least one other piece of material that showed her birth date.

Most of this had to go to some office in suburban Trenton, our state capital, to be processed, and Ella would not even be allowed to practice until she was cleared. Ella and I went to watch the next weekend as this team, having only ten healthy players, got tromped by some neighboring town. Still unprocessed, Ella had to sit out another week, another game with only ten players.

This would have been funny if it weren't so annoying. Earlier that year, we were about to set off on a trip to Spain on a Sunday night flight when, the evening before, Sue just happened to look at Sylvia's passport to discover it had expired. Seemingly desperate, she called the State Department, and the person there said that if we went down to Washington on Sunday morning with a couple of pieces of relevant information, we could renew Sylvia's passport. Ella and I got up early for the two-and-a-half-hour drive, sat in a waiting room for about thirty minutes, and came back with the passport. So the check on us to go to Spain was significantly less than Ella's B team background grilling.

By mid-October, Ella was finally on the field, running up and down with abandon. What was amazing about it all was that it seemed like a lot of fun. At least at this point, the B teamers did not consider themselves lesser characters than their A team superiors. A missed kick or a dribbler that got by the defense and goalie elicited a shrug. A goal was a source of joy and a chance to gather as many hugs as time would allow.

At this juncture Ella's greatest skills were never slowing down and, perhaps because she was the smallest kid on the field, a propensity for getting fouled, especially by the least coordinated and largest members of the other team. One early November afternoon, as the temperature was sinking and the wind was revving up on the secondary Crows Woods field—a rutted and hilly affair suitable only for B teams—Ella took the ball near the back end line and dribbled furiously through the ranks of the other team down the right side. Her head was down and focused on the ball most of the time, and she didn't so much deke the opponents as weave, obviously determined, past them. At the end of the run, she found, maybe to her surprise, a tall but gawky girl barreling parallel to her about 30 feet closer to the goal mouth. She gave everything she had to the kick across—which, at 4-foot-whatever-she-was, still was an effort—directly onto the girl's right foot, which somehow directed the ball into the goal.

This goal came just minutes after Jack O'Malley showed up to watch a few minutes of the game. Jack is the icon for all that is virtuous about youth sports, be it in Haddonfield or wherever else he could be. Though he travels for work, he has been the coach at every level of every sport there is, sometimes in the absence of his own kids on the team. Jack grew up in Haddonfield and grew just tall enough to be pretty good at all sports then, if not quite the star of any team. After college at Dickinson, a really good liberal arts school about three hours to the west, he returned to town to raise his three kids and influence dozens more as a coach. He never misses the Haddonfield fire truck when, bound by tradition, it carries the many high school state championship teams (there were an unbelievable seven state championships Ella's high school senior year) through town as soon as they return from the meet or game that brought them a championship. When he can, Jack actually gets to all those state championship games and shows up at random wrestling matches and swim meets and, as here, B girls' soccer games.

At that moment, though, Jack was coaching the vaunted fifth-grade girls' A team.

"Wow," he told me during halftime. "I didn't know Ella had that in her. I didn't think she even played."

"Well, I don't . . ." was all I could get out.

"Let me have her. She's just what we need. Spunk," he said. "Hey, got to go to a fall baseball game. Talk to you later."

My mouth was still in the fourth word of that first sentence, not that I knew exactly what it would be. I didn't even get a chance to wave before Jack was gathering his sons, Johnny and Patrick, and bounding toward his van.

It didn't matter, though. There was joy coming to Mudville. With her mad dash, Ella had blown by that B Reaper. Hallelujah and all those blessings: She was going to be an A team girl.

When we started visiting colleges in Ella's junior year of high school, she became enamored of the University of Virginia. It is hard not to love the campus at first sight, its buildings and landscaping designed originally by Thomas Jefferson on the model of his own estate, Monticello, and other classical influences.

In addition to that, Ella loved that UVA had traditions galore, some of which involved secret societies and the need for arcane knowledge. Kids from UVA, she perceived, had a sense of themselves as not quite superior but certainly different in a positive, confident manner.

The whole effect reminded me of the concept of the A team. Sometimes, it almost seemed as if you needed to know secret handshakes or arcane passwords to be a part of it. It was as if there were an alumni network of older kids and their parents who were A team material. Perhaps, it seemed, it was not even about skill but about genetics—or maybe eugenics.

Like with any second kid, parents think they learn hints and secrets about handling similar situations from how they handled the first one. Dr. Spock promised us this in his seminal book about child care.

But Dr. Spock obviously ignored those A and B youth soccer tryouts—an egregious omission—in his research.

Sylvia's body type, not to mention her overall demeanor, was not at all Ella's. Sylvia ended up being about 4 inches taller than Ella, but what's more significant is that her whole aspect is softer and rounder. Sylvia was never fat, but Ella is hard-boned and muscled, even in her diminutiveness, so Sylvia will always look pudgy in comparison. Furthermore, she is about as white as they make them, burning at even the thought of overhead sun. She bears no resemblance to the Mellman side of the family, my mother's. Everyone there had black hair, wavy or curly or even Jew-fro. My mother's 1928 high school graduation photo makes her look like an African American flapper. I inherited her dark skin, which, conversely, tans deeply at the mention of even a summer breeze. Though my doctors admonish me to always wear hats and long sleeves, my daughters are livid when they see me practically sepia by mid-April.

So every time Sylvia tried out for sports as a young-un, coaches saw this full-cheeked kid with almost a pallor and figured she could hardly be lithe and quick. Rather than resigning herself to be a defender or a rebounder or a shot-putter or some other round-person position, Sylvia wisely chose to be a goalie, or its equivalent, instead. Few girls wanted the tension of goaliedom, especially in those delicate adolescent years. Sylvia had a ho-hum acceptance of it.

Playing goalie often got her out of running, Sylvia realized, especially in soccer. When they run out of things to instruct, youth soccer coaches make kids do a lap or two around the field. As an ex–high school cross-country guy, I can say that running is wonderful exercise, but kids in preteen soccer hardly need it. These kids are running from the moment they get up until they conk out at night. When they "run" around a field, they tend to use that as a way to goof around. They chat with one another, or they jump on one another, or they see how slow they can go, or just go fast so they can rest up at the end.

Sylvia discovered this early on and figured she would hang out at the net and not bother running at all. Even if a coach gave her two or three practice kicks during the around-the-field run, she was that much better off at learning some skill than the kids doing about 0.03 percent of their running for the day.

To be fair, Sylvia's grade of girls was full of soccer standouts. Early on, many of them started playing year-round: winter indoor leagues, two teams in the spring and fall, summer camps in Indiana or Virginia or maybe Guantánamo, where military operatives let sequestered inmates pay off their debts to society by giving U.S. prodigies secrets from their soccer-sodden homelands.

Since Sylvia played "only" on fall and spring teams, and despite the alleged objectiveness of soccer tryout judges, she was always on the margins during those tryouts, held in May for teams that would start in September. Furthermore, the results were not revealed until school was over, about a month later. I think those results were kept in the same vaults as the voting for the Academy Awards. The ostensible reason was that kids who were deemed A team material would lord it over the degraded B kids during schooltime. Waiting until summer, the Soccer Potentates presumed, would prevent some kind of civil war among Haddonfield youth.

The absurdity of this was compounded by the reality that the decision the Potentates were making was between, at most, five kids a grade. It was clear who was really good and who was on the back end, so it was only the middle few who needed separating. Sometimes I helped on the basketball judging, and we usually posted that within a couple of days, waiting that long just to make sure. Swimming, running, and the like were ranked instantly, by times recorded at the trials.

Soccer Potentates believe they are like a Senate subcommittee or maybe a Cold War Soviet cabal. The more time they take to announce their findings, the more important their sport is, and hence they are. Popes, junta leaders, even sovereign nations have taken less time to be confirmed than A and B teams in the Haddonfield Soccer Fiefdom. At least a couple of times, the absurdity caught the Strauss girls in the swirl.

The year Ella got pulled up to the A soccer team, some of the girls thought they did so well that they decided to eschew the Haddonfield teams altogether and play in towns where the teams were even better for seventh grade. In addition, the B team coaches asked their girls to ignore tryouts and stick with the Bs, since they could move up in competition for the next year anyway.

Those decisions were all part of the kudzu-like spreading of the youth soccer hegemony. In addition to this long secretive A and B decision making, there is a whole South Jersey Soccer Association to deal with. I am certain there are similar groups covering every acre of at least the Lower Forty-Eight, no doubt a southwestern South Dakota and a northeastern North Dakota one. So this association meets, coven-like, before every season to rank the teams within. To some parents, playing in the Olympic or Tippy-Top or Gigantor, or whatever they call the division with the presumed six or eight best teams in the region is like playing UCLA basketball when John Wooden was winning all those championships. I am sure the kids like it, but since the association covens deciding which teams are superior are all made up of parents—not a kid in sight—it is those parents who live to be Tippy-Top or Gigantor.

So this particular year, the fallout from the girls leaving the A team and the presumed reupping of the entire B got the two teams only two divisions apart. Except that in the end, everyone did go to tryouts. Ella seemed to be secure on the A squad, but when the squads were posted the day after sixth grade ended, her A wings were shredded. Four girls came up from the B, and she was the lone descender.

For people of relative sanity, all of this is about as meaningless as a butterfly flapping its wings on a balmy spring day. But that butterfly fluttering can cause air waves that eventually build into a typhoon off the island of Guam. The next B year was one to wallow in. Maybe in fourth grade, parents and kids were sanguine about their B-ness, but by middle school, almost anyone who hadn't abandoned the sport was livid about the placement.

I don't remember the exact record of that seventh-grade B team, but I do remember driving a whole bunch of miles with three or four girls doing everything but putting Amish hexes on referees and desperately trying to appease coaches. The A team was going on to the Gigantor championship, as I remember, but this B thing was only heading toward a psychiatrist's couch.

Miraculously, Ella made the A team in eighth grade, another Haddonfield girl having gone off to play in some more soccer-worthy town. She scored a couple of goals by season's end and, after the last game, made a speech to the other girls, thanking them for their wonderful teammateness, that Jack O'Malley said had tears streaming down from his eyes.

Despite the opportunity to be on the edges of a team that eventually won two state high school championships, Ella knew how to go out on top, that being her last competitive soccer game. She gave her speech, finishing one segment of her young sporting life.

Somehow, I was able to endure the girls' A- and B-ness in basketball better than I had in soccer, maybe because there were funnier moments, or because they were able to find their roles on those teams.

We were away for Christmas in Michigan at Sue's parents' house that fifth-grade winter, so Ella just got placed on a team, and she would have her first game in a tournament when we returned just before the New Year. Frankly, at this point I really did not know A from B, since all the teams before were picked, I figured, on the basis of friendships or at random.

When we got to the tournament at the cavernous Blue Barn, an indoor athletic complex built by a nearby municipality in the flush years of the tech bubble, there was Jack O'Malley waiting with his usual smile. This couldn't be a bad thing. Jack played basketball in high school. I didn't want to coach. Ella got to wear number 3, for her then-favorite, Allen Iverson. Heaven.

"Welcome to the B team, girls," Jack started his pregame pep talk. Then he went into his usual sardonic humor. "The object is to score a little bit more than the other girls over there. Everyone will get to play, assuming her shoes are tied and her uniform isn't on inside out."

By default, being the shortest and actually being able to dribble the ball, Ella got to be point guard. It turned out that she was the one who could shoot. In the first few games, Ella made half the team's points. This wasn't the triumph that it seemed, since it meant that she would score 8 in a 30–16 loss or 10 in a 42–20 drubbing.

It was clear that in Ella's absence there had been tryouts of a sort, and B meant not one of two equal teams but one of presumed lesser skill. I began to call Ella Queen B, for her scoring and sometimes for her imperiousness in telling the other kids what to do.

Yet what I found wonderful about the Bs was that the parents, absolved of expectations, were willing to cheer for everyone. Sometimes—though this sounds crazy—parents root against the girls on their kids' teams and root, albeit silently, for the girls on the other. If a kid on Ella's team screws up, then maybe Ella will get more playing time. Or, maybe, if Ella really is a deserved second-teamer, if the other team scores enough, she will get in all the more, albeit in a lost cause.

In B-dom, there is clearly less of that. Even in her time as Queen B, Ella was still only a B girl. Jack knew the wisdom of having ten-year-olds spend time on the court, even if they didn't really tie their shoes for him or could barely loft the ball basketward.

"Michael Jordan got cut his sophomore year" was the B byword. True or not, that oft-intoned line has no doubt saved a lot of wailing from kids cut from A teams all over American suburbia. Frankly, I never believed it, and if it were true, Jordan was probably already off making underwear commercials instead of jamming one through the hoop.

Ella did have a couple of defining moments as Queen B. There was the time that she made a steal in the backcourt and started dribbling upcourt with abandon. As she was on her approach to the hoop, taking that first Jordanesque liftoff step, her mouth guard fell floorward. Undeterred, she kept going up with the ball in her right hand. She reached down simultaneously with her left hand and caught the mouth guard in midflight. Without even a flinch, as if this were a play she had seen on a coaching video, she continued in flight and made the layup.

For years afterwards, the ref at that game, if he were officiating another of her games, would see her as he came to the gym and squeal, "Mouth Guard, how's it going?"

Ella was always the shortest kid around, something that she often lamented. It only enhanced her cuteness, but it did little to create a first impression on any basketball coach.

Each season, she would have to grunt and groan and prove once again that, yes, she could shoot the three-pointer, do a crossover dribble, and defend against kids far taller than she. Mostly she just bore with it, but I know it could not have been a pleasant task.

At least early on, though, her being short brought more funny moments than disappointing ones. There was the time in fifth or sixth grade when Ella grabbed onto a ball that the tallest kid from Haddon Township was gripping. The other girl did her best to wrest it from Ella, who would not let up her grip. Finally, the girl just lifted the ball above her head, but Ella, as if in a cartoon, still didn't let go and flew up with the ball. The girl then slammed it back down and Ella, now back on the ground, with her knees only slightly bent, kept her clutch firm. The girl flew her up again, her long arms at their highest reach, but Ella, now at least 18 inches off the ground, kept on it like Stick-em.

The refs were obviously choked up in laughter, since they didn't blow their whistles for a jump ball. Finally, the girl just threw the ball down, a disgusted fling. Ella still had it, now on her butt, and calmly tossed it to her teammate as if it had been a scripted play.

We have another photo, taken about this age, of Ella in a too-large sea-blue T-shirt, the short sleeves hiked up to her shoulders. She was playing in the intermediate girls' league run by the Stone Harbor recreation department in the South Jersey Shore town where we have a summer house. She had her arms out in a perfect defensive stance, and her eyes were homed in on the ball being dribbled by a tall blond girl with long, frizzy hair.

Though you can see only the back of the girl in the photo, we are convinced that this is pop star Taylor Swift. Swift's family used to have a house in Stone Harbor, and when I interviewed her once for a story, I asked her whether she played in the summer basketball rec program, which she vaguely remembered doing because, she said, she tried just about anything to meet kids during her then-shy years.

When Sylvia's fifth-grade basketball tryout came, she was ready, having been dragged to dozens of Ella's games. She made the A team as the designated shooter, off and on as a starter, but definitely in the rotation. Sylvia learned how to shoot a basketball so well, I think, to avoid the dreaded "suicides" that youth coaches always seemed to want to do at the end of basketball practices. In Haddonfield, the suicide is a sprint to the foul line and back to the baseline, then to half court and back, then to three-quarter court and back, then the whole shebang. It is just about the worst thing you can do at the end of a practice since it tightens you up just when you should be stretching out and cooling off. I have never seen a youth coach order stretching at the end of even the hardest practice, and since all of this stuff seems handed down, my bet is that Sylvia's daughters will be doing suicides at the end of fifth-grade travel basketball.

In any case, the one way to thwart a suicide call is for a selected shooter to make a foul shot or some combination of shots. Practices traditionally end with the coach calling some girl out to shoot, and if she makes the requisite shot or shots, practice ends and said girl is lauded with hero hugs.

Whatever Sylvia may have lacked in speed or dexterity, she was always the best shooter for several grades up and down from hers. From the time she was eight, she could make three-pointers steadily, and she almost never lost a foul-shooting contest; her most significant win was at the Penn State summer camp when she was ten, where she won several T-shirts.

So when suicide prevention came up at the end of every basketball practice, the girls often beseeched the coach to choose Sylvia as the shooter. Even the better shooters would do this, since the pressure to make the shot was high, and they coveted friendships. In addition to her shooting prowess, Sylvia was an ice queen, her goalkeeping in other seasons perhaps adding to her calm in this situation.

Her practice-ending mystique was a source of silent pride for me. It inevitably happened just as parents came for pickup, so what little they saw of practice was often a Sylvia swish from the foul or three-point line. It was undeniable and positive. When Sylvia finally quit basketball at the beginning of the freshman season in high school, the other parents were baffled. No matter whether they thought their daughters were better overall than Sylvia, they couldn't believe the girl who had always kept their kids suicide-free had left what seemed to be her calling.

The apprenticeships, for both the girls and Dad, were nearing an end, though. Middle school and high school sports were coming, where overbearing parents would have to slip away from the coaching boxes and, presumably, skill and character would win out. There would be more choices, too, and my girls had already had their minds attuned to them.

Sporting
Transitions
The Last Innocent Years

Sometime while Ella was in middle school, we went to a Haddonfield girls' high school basketball game, just for a night together. Ella was watching through the first half, but I could see there was something else on her mind. Had she discovered boys? Was there an imminent Harry Potter release I didn't know about? Her look was hard, and she was constantly biting the inside of her lower lip.

"You know, Dad," she finally said with the air of pronouncement, "I think I have figured out what sports I am going to play in high school."

I gulped. High school was more than three years away, a third of her life still ahead. On the other hand, I was fascinated by what might come out. It turned out to be almost a complete surprise.

"I am going to play tennis in the fall, basketball in the winter, and crew in the spring," she said, always looking forward, then finally releasing the bite of her lip and nodding her head sharply for finality.

I didn't react immediately, at least outwardly. I don't remember how the game turned out, though to be sure, Haddonfield's girls were perennial basketball winners, so I am fairly certain it was to the good.

Though I said nothing, I tried to parse Ella's definitive declaration in my mind. Basketball, yes, that seemed obvious, given that she had been shooting them up for years by this time. Tennis? Well, she had done some winter indoor thing at one of the elementary schools. The instructor gave out candy at the end of the sessions, so maybe that was the Haddonfield youth equivalent to high tea at Wimbledon.

But crew?

The Cooper River—actually an estuary acting more like a lake—is about 2 miles from our house, and a bridge over it is a crossing on the short route to Philadelphia and Camden. In the 1960s, Jack Kelly Jr., Princess Grace of Monaco's brother and an Olympic rower, had led a project to make it into a rowing center, and in the ensuing years it had become the place where the Olympic trials, college national championships, and dozens of major regattas have taken place. Ella probably had been looking from her back seat perch at the shells dramatically going past as I swerved around traffic, blinkered to the Cooper's picturesqueness.

Fortuitously, Haddonfield High School began its crew club just as Ella was reaching middle school. A few of her basketball friends, particularly the taller and stronger ones, answered the first call for a summer middle school rowing class at the Cooper. Ella, who was already one of those ballplayers who directly, if mostly pleasantly, told her teammates what to do in all her other sports, had heard there was this position, coxswain, where the only real requirement was to do that.

"Oh, my gosh, this is wonderful," said the woman running the class when Ella showed up. Ella came there at the same time as one of her friends, who was already nearing 6 feet at age thirteen. The woman looked up and down at Katie and smiled approvingly. Then she looked, mostly down, at Ella, who was not approaching much more than four-and-a-half feet, just as approvingly.

I could see the confidence radiating. Finally, a sport where height didn't matter and diminutiveness, at least in one position, was prized. It is not at all likely that when Ella had chosen crew several years before, she realized she would fit so snugly into it.

About the same time, while Ella was starting her coxswain career based at the shell storage area on the north side of the Cooper, Sylvia decided, on the suggestion of our next-door neighbor Dana, that she would take sailing lessons with Dana's son, David, out of the small marina on the south side.

Given the changes that were swimming about in our household, it hardly seemed propitious that Ella and Sylvia were going aquatic. I was mostly oblivious to Sylvia's turn, since at the time I had to go out to Los Angeles for work for a while. I am now especially saddened that I was not there for the climactic last day of class.

As Sue tells it, Sylvia was practically a Ted-Turner-at-the-America's-Cup character. On the last day of class, the instructors encouraged the students to invite parents into the sailboat for a trip up and down the Cooper. Sylvia was in her training helmet and lifejacket and looked askance at her friends David and Mark, who were laughing and fooling around like the preteen boys they were.

Sylvia directed Sue to a seat and told her to be calm. Sue was not the sailing type, but she figured she would have to monitor her nine-year-old daughter a bit. As they went out tacking and mark-twaining and whatever else sailboats do, Sue shifted a bit to grab a pole or something she thought useful, until the admonishment started.

"Sit. Down. Mommy," came the sharp reply as Sylvia directed the sail with her right arm ramrod straight. Sue tried to be helpful in a deferential tone, but she got the words again, with a flick of the hand down and a pointing finger: "Sit. Down. Mommy."

This time Sue scrambled back to her seat, from then on following instructions from Captain Bluebeard, or whoever this fresh-faced sailor had become.

Unfortunately, that was the last of Sylvia aft, astern, starboard, or port. She has always had her goals in sports, and when she reaches them, the end often comes abruptly. For instance, the big summer diving meet in these parts is called Tri-County, since it involves the swim clubs from Gloucester County to the south and Burlington County to the north of our home, Camden County. Each year, the Tri-County diving cabal takes, I believe, tea leaf samplings from secret plantings along the Hwang Ho River and comes up with a scoring number for each age group that will qualify a kid for the vaunted Tri-County meet.

For her first four years, Sylvia did not come remotely near that number in any preliminary meet. Yet her goal each year was to get to Tri-County. Practice after practice, flawed dive after flawed dive, she muddled through. I could understand because I have the same gene. Most people, I believe, choose hobbies at which they are at least moderately decent. Makes sense, does it not? I know a guy who makes duck carvings. They aren't Rodin sculptures, but they are pretty good, at least worthy of being shown on mantelpieces and shelves all over his house. My friends play whatever games they do, from bridge to chess to tennis, with the reasonable expectation that they will win. My gardening friends always show off their latest beautiful plants or bring over their prize tomatoes. My friend Bill, who spends countless hours fishing, has given us freezerfuls of scrumptious seafood year after year.

These people are sane. They spend whatever leisure time they have doing something that pats the ego and ends up in productive, admirable, and satisfying results.

Sylvia and I, though, often spend our leisure hours doing things we are not particularly good at. Despite all the trophies that line her shelf, Sylvia was, minute spent for minute spent, a pretty wretched diver. For most of the last thirty years, I have played basketball about four or five times a week, often more. I am still usually the worst guy on any basketball court. When I am part of the contingent shooting to see who gets to play next, there is always a conflicted soul watching. He is the guy who is already on the team who genuinely likes me and absolutely despises the other guy shooting for that last spot. Still, there is little within him that wants me to make that shot. No matter what logic says, there are times when the choice can be the Devil over Mother Teresa, and if Lucifer could pick quarters off the top of the backboard, that would be it.

The summer after her sailing class, I feared that in Sylvia's Tri-County diving quest she had picked an unattainable goal. I figured I would be wheeling in from the nursing home, the oxygen tank soldered to my motorized chair, watching forty-six-year-old Sylvia still trying to perfect a back dive, determined to overcome all odds to be the most ancient Tri-Countier.

Then, wonder of wonders, miracle of miracles, the tea leaves on the Hwang Ho had a bountiful season. In her fifth diving year, the qualification score for Tri-County slithered significantly downward. With one fairly decent inward dive in the early morning at the five-way meet in the hollow of the Haddon Heights glen area swim club, a sympathetic and probably sun-addled judge gave Sylvia a 5½, boosting her score to qualify for the Tri-County meet by mere tenths of a point. The blue snow had fallen and the moon was made of green cheese. In her perverseness, she had conquered. At Tri-County, she came in twenty-fourth out of, I think, twenty-seven in her age group.

Since that day, she has never so much as whispered the words "back dive" in any public forum I know about. She has not even sat in a sailboat again as far as I can tell. The day after she made first-chair clarinet in the school orchestra, she "lost" the clarinet, case and all. Her first and only perfect cartwheel came the same day as her last gymnastics class.

Sylvia is an uncommon kid. As I have noted, I hope she studies Samuel Beckett someday, because she could be one of his characters. If the true athlete and competitor revels primarily in the quest, then Sylvia is the truest of the true.

Then again, that only makes her Daddy's girl exactly: contrarian to the max.

I am guessing my parents shelled out a good hundred dollars on my entire youth sporting career. Most of it had to be in sneakers, which in a good year meant Chuck Taylor Converse and most others something out of the bin at the local discount stores, what we kids called W.T. Grant specials.

I think I had a grand total of three baseball gloves in the dozen or so years I played in the sandlots. Each time my dad bought a new one, he stuck a baseball in the pocket, wrapped twine around the whole thing, and shmeared a mysterious substance called neatsfoot oil on the glove, like cream cheese on a bagel. Neatsfoot oil, I read later, was made from the shinbone of a calf and was a primary agent in Colonial times for softening leather. My father was a history buff, so I am guessing he read about it in one of his many tomes: a biography of Gouverneur Morris or my Delaware buddy Caesar Rodney or some other minor Founding Father. The glove then lay dormant for a week or so before he would let me use it. I have to admit, it was pretty soft by the time I got to play with it—so soft, sometimes, that the ball would fall out of the webbing.

I had one whole tennis racket for the entirety of my high school career and one basketball, which somehow remained intact for those same four years of high school.

Sylvia could go through my father's entire lifetime expenditure on my athletic career, cauldron of neatsfoot oil included, in one weekend lacrosse tournament. Annually, whatever summer team she happens to be on goes to a weekend lacrosse fiesta in central New Jersey's horse country called Lax for the Cure. Although I do not doubt the sincerity of the organizers to hope for the end of breast cancer, this is the kind of thing that exists mainly for every girl with a lacrosse stick from Massachusetts to North Carolina to buy every conceivable clothing item in pink, a color that seems incongruous for a sport that revels in black and blue. It is a land of $25 T-shirts and $28 shorts, not to mention mouth guards and hair ribbons and lanyards and shoelaces and things that go in piercings that, frankly, I do not want to know about.

Yet Lax for the Cure and its like are just the culmination of the play-for-pay culture of today's kiddie sports world. From the time Ella got that first purple T-shirt on that first biddie soccer team, I believe I have paid the equivalent of the gross national product of a medium-sized European nation for equipment, clothing, fees, and travel for Ella's and Sylvia's sports. Manchester United, the British soccer franchise, is said to be the most valuable on the planet, worth something like

$1.6 billion. There's a vague possibility that the resale value of the sporting paraphernalia in my girls' closets approaches that.

I was on the beach one day, a summer respite in the late 1990s, chatting with a veteran sports dad from the home neighborhood. He beckoned me over like the man did to Benjamin Braddock (Dustin Hoffman) in the famous pool scene in *The Graduate*. Instead of "plastics," that dad said sub rosa, "AAU." Though not the key to financial success that Benjamin sought, AAU is the Yellow Brick Road to the Oz of youth sports in the current age, and from that moment I realized Ella and Sylvia were bound to tread on it, guidance from the Scarecrow, Tin Man, and Cowardly Lion notwithstanding. There was status to be gained and money to be spent: uniforms, travel, real referees, and, presumably, glory at the end of the Emerald Checkbook.

Ostensibly, the Amateur Athletic Union is a clearinghouse or sanctioning body for amateur noncollegiate and non–high school sports. In reality, it is a racket that even Al Capone would have loved to control. Like the kingdom, phylum, order, family, genus, species, and so forth hierarchy of the animal universe, kids sports generally goes upward from Sandlot to Town, Travel, and AAU, and the cost to parents rises exponentially along the way, though the psychic and physical benefit is said to be worth the ticket.

When Ella thought she was good enough, she asked us to seek out an AAU basketball team that she could try out for. The tryouts would be in March, with the season starting in April and weekend tournaments ruining—er, played on weekends through the early summer.

So at age ten, she went to the tryouts for the Penn–Jersey Panthers. Unfortunately, she played a masterful team game, picking and passing and taking the best girl on defense, no matter that she was inches taller and twice as fast. She took charges from girls 30 pounds heavier and tried desperately to save balls slicing out of bounds.

She did not come close to making the team.

A sardonic sage once said, "The race does not always go to the swift, nor the battle to the strong, but that, sir, is the place to park your money." The fact is that, especially if you are tiny, you had better score a hodload of points or you are not going to move an AAU coach's eyes your way.

By the next year, though, Ella had made the Panthers, and that really revved up our check writing. A uniform, coaches' fees, practice venue rental, and several tournaments were about $400 a kid. Then each tournament had a commemorative T-shirt the kids all got sullen about if you did not ante up. There were Cokes and sandwiches between games; mostly these tournaments have four or five games on a couple of consecutive days. The coup de grace comes when a team decides to take an overnight road trip, as Ella's sixth-grade AAU team did to Newport, Rhode Island. Newport is the home of some of the largest seaside mansions in the country, and our hotel charges were similarly exorbitant.

Ah, but it is all worth it, or so they say. Instead of Ella playing against kids in her own neighborhood or maybe just a couple of towns away, she got to play against kids with similarly wallet-sucked-dry parents from places just far away enough so they have to pay for overnights and overpriced dinners as well. These teams are always called something intimidating and obscure, like the D-1-Lightning or the Red Hurricanes or the Southside Barside Barracudas. Supposedly, the girls will be playing level age-group competition, but there are invariably blowouts on either side, so the idea of playing "better" competition is usually a myth. Had any of the teams just split up evenly and found a hoop to play at, even half court, they would probably progress just as well.

Yet the system is founded on excess.

I admit being sucked in at times.

When Sylvia played on her first AAU basketball team at age ten, she was the second highest scorer the first few games out. I reveled in thinking she was the bee's knees, or some other animalistic superiority. I even told Sue that I had responsibilities as the parent of a star. I would have to act humbly, complimenting often the play of lesser girls, graciously accepting kudos about my daughter's regular court accomplishments.

Then they played in the local Lizzie Haddon Mother's Day tournament. In the first game, Sylvia's team was shoveled into a mismatch with a team from a county or so away.

At the end of that game, I sidled over to Sylvia and put my arm on her shoulder.

"I am proud of you for being the high scorer," I told her, affecting humility. "Unfortunately, you only scored one point."

Had not a girl from the other team mistakenly fouled Sylvia as the first half wound down and she was taking the buzzer-beater, Sylvia's team, an alleged AAU supersquad, would have been blanked, zeroed, goose-egged, zilched. That AAU season, I think I got away with only about $600 in fees and paraphernalia. Sylvia came away with, I think, three victorious games out of twenty.

It is at these AAU and other off-season sport tournaments that the whispering starts about college recruiting. There are courts and fields full of kids in regalia and parents biting their fingernails and trading rumors.

"See the guy over there? The one in the sunglasses. I hear he's the Duke reserve deputy adjunct assistant coach." "No, no, I saw him yesterday in a Hofstra shirt." "I am sure he's Duke. Well, anyway, my kid scored a whole bunch when he watched."

That he probably was the ice cream vendor taking a quick break couldn't have deterred any determined parent. That it is parents of sixth graders thinking this way is insane. Suffice it to say, though, that the likes of Julius "Dr. J" Erving or Babe Ruth or Jim Brown or any of the great innovators in sports would not have had the opportunity to be playground creative in the AAU-type tournament system. Erving's flying slam-dunks and Ruth's swinging at the heels would have been coached out. Dick Fosbury, the inventor of the "Fosbury Flop" high jump method used by all top competitive jumpers over the last thirty years, practiced the move after hours at high school. He probably would have stayed jumping 5 feet, instead of more than 7 feet, had he listened to his summer coaches, who insisted he stay with the straddle method.

Another way to spend good cash in youth sports is to send the kid to a college camp. This way, he or she gets time with college coaches and players, who allegedly know more about teaching ten-year-olds their skills than your average dad or mom. In reality, it is mostly a way for schools to fill up dormant summer dorm space with cash-paying customers and a way for athletes and coaches to make some money without the NCAA coming in to crack heads. It also gives parents a way to indulge their sports-saturated kids even more. I have a buddy whose older kid loved Duke and whose younger one admired the University of North Carolina. He indulged both. Unfortunately, the basketball camps at these places ran consecutive weeks, so he shlepped one the nine hours to Durham and back, picked up the other, and did the same to Chapel Hill.

Fortunately, when Ella's basketball-playing friends decided they needed a camp, they chose Penn State, a mere four hours each way. They got the privilege of staying in high-rise dorms of dubious quality and no air conditioning. At eleven or twelve, though, that in itself was an attraction. So, apparently, was some male assistant coach, who seems to be in every photograph we have of that camp, a bit too close to those pubescent girls. The next year, Ella went back to Penn State for tennis, where she claimed she learned a serve during the week she was there. She rushed me over to the local courts immediately after returning home and blooped me moon-balls for the next half hour, proud that they were going in the box at least. Only $500 for the opportunity to see me cringe because some opponent could blast those serves back into her gullet.

Still, the lack of actual sporting progress in Ella's college instruction did not deter Sylvia from wanting to stay in those dilapidated high-rise dorms at Penn State the summer after fifth grade. She knew just whom she wanted to come with her, and as soon as I gave approval in April for the early July camp, she got on the phone. A few days later, the mom called me in a downcast voice. The girl had told her that since she was on the B team, she wasn't good enough to go to a camp, that she would never be good enough, and that just the thought of it all was probably going to make her quit basketball.

Sylvia had apparently pleaded with her, telling her stories from her sister about the amazing ice cream in the cafeteria— Penn State has its own creamery where ice cream shop owners go for refresher courses—and the half day at the university swimming pool. The mom had a quiver in her voice, and I got a little teary myself.

The curse of the B team had come to life to ruin a fun five days away from parents. Sylvia knew the drill. Basketball was just an excuse. Ice cream and goofing around in a college dorm was the point. But the girl had decided. Her basketball career was over at age ten. She was a B, and that is all she would ever be, Penn State or no. So Penn State was a no.

Sylvia went to the camp with another girl, and the morning it was to be over, she called me early to tell me to get up there for the award ceremony at noon. I gathered up my Aunt Erma, the only Penn State alum in our family, and scorched up to University Park in a record three and a half hours, running into the Bryce Jordan Center with no time to lose. Sylvia had won all those shooting contests and kept getting T-shirts from then–Penn State coach Rene Portland, who seemed to be sizing up the not-so-sizable Sylvia at each T-shirt awarding.

Sylvia, though, was less impressed with herself, or at least the sharpshooting part of herself. She threw the T-shirts at me and ran to the cafeteria, wanting only to make sure she could get one more Penn State ice cream before the ride home.

"Next year, she is coming," Sylvia demanded, alluding to her career-over-at-ten friend. "We'll find another sport. I'll even swim. She can't miss the ice cream anymore."

Now there's a sporting lesson that Babe Ruth, the gourmand athlete, would have loved.

High School
A Lot of Sweet and a Bit of Bitter

There they were, eight small bags, perched on the dining room settee like a still life in Kodachrome. The mauve one, emblazoned "Allie" across its front, had green tissue paper popping out from the top. To its right was a red bag, marked "Emily," with yellow tissue atop. The next was orange, with blue paper and "Annie," followed by those marked "Erica" (yellow bag with orange tissue), "Sarah" (green bag with red tissue), "Maria" (blue bag with tangerine tissue), "Jackie" (navy bag with scarlet tissue), and finally "Kendall" (indigo bag with multicolored tissue).

The bags, filled with matching-colored T-shirts, inspired Sue to name their recipients "The RainBoat," the Haddonfield Memorial High School 2008 girls' lightweight eight, getting ready to head to the U.S. Rowing National Championship Regatta in Oak Ridge, Tennessee.

The summer before, just after her freshman year, Ella was on the South Jersey Rowing Club, and in the club nationals she coxed a boat that won a bronze medal, third behind a couple of Junior Olympic training boats out of Washington. The results made the local newspaper, and I cut them out and had them mounted at the trophy shop.

Ella was appropriately disdainful, but Sue told her, "No Strauss or Warner has ever been in a national anything. It may never happen again. At least let Daddy feel good about it."

Ella's high school crew coach was not happy with kids who did winter sports and did not attend his winter workouts. Even though she was going to be a coxswain—and therefore not in need of rowing-machine training—and had done the middle school summer programs, when he would see her, he chided her for playing basketball and tennis in the winter and fall. She tried to placate him by coming to the Saturday morning workouts when he had them.

One particularly cold Saturday morning that freshman winter, she asked me to drop her off at the elementary school playground. The crew girls were going running, and she felt compelled to be there. I didn't hear from her for nearly two hours and got a little worried. She tromped back in the house, though, cheeks flushed and slush caressing her sneakers.

"How'd it go?" I asked warily.

"No one else showed up," she muttered. "Waited a long time. Did a few laps and a few streets. Could you make me a hot chocolate? I've got basketball in an hour."

Despite this and two more Saturday morning workouts, the coach still got on her about basketball when the spring season started. She never got a chance at coxing the lead freshman boat, but since a bunch of her friends were on the second boat, it didn't seem to faze her all that much.

Crew is a strange sort of cult. Its partisans intone, almost religiously, that it is the ultimate team sport, where all the members of the boat have to pull together or the ship, metaphorically, sinks.

That's a whole bunch of hooey. I have never seen or heard of a kid who is the strongest- or fastest-stroking rower not being on the top boat because he or she might be somewhat out of sync with the other rowers. Frankly, that would have been like excluding Babe Ruth from the lineup in the early 1920s because he was hitting home runs when everyone else was only pussyfooting with singles and doubles.

So although the coach could have—and since they were all novices as freshmen, should have—put the girls on two equal, in-sync boats, that was not the way it was. Inevitably, the stronger girls who got on the top boat got better, and they got better still when the coaches concentrated on them to the exclusion of Ella's boat. As in any other team, the race is to the strong and swift, and the parents and kids would be upset if it were any other way.

Still, the freshman season ended amicably, and lots of kids returned the next year. The coach looked around and saw a lot of young, smaller girls and started a lightweight boat. The girls needed to weigh 130 pounds or less, something not hard for even muscled sixteen-year-olds.

Haddonfield being an ambitious town, when the coach got a slew of boats qualified for the nationals, parents were ready at the checkbook to ante up for a Memorial Day weekend trip to Tennessee. I did my best to defray some costs and arranged a story to write on some second-home village in the Great Smoky Mountains, not far from Oak Ridge.

Those Great Smokies may seem like an incongruous place to have a national championship in what may be the most monied and snobby sport short of polo, but it does come with a strange history.

In the mid-twentieth century, Oak Ridge was the home of intensive—and mostly secret—atomic energy research. Things were so secret, in fact, that roads approaching the town suddenly veered around it. The head of the city's chamber of commerce told me that into the 1960s, Oak Ridge school sports teams had no names, and often no numbers, on uniforms, lest it be known that the dad or mom of Player X was an Oak Ridge scientist.

Lots of those scientists came from Ivy League universities, and in their heydays they had rowed for the likes of Harvard, Princeton, Yale, and Dartmouth, still among the elite in college rowing circles. The Tennessee Valley Authority had dammed up rivers, making some lakes suitable for rowing just nearby, so although few other places within hours of driving had any crew clubs, the Oak Ridgers had theirs.

So the Haddonfield Crew Club rented a bus for the two-day trip down to Tennessee, an unprecedented jaunt for a local school team that, I think, required approval of just about every governing body in town.

When I met the kids and weary chaperones at the Motel 6 in nearby Knoxville, the assistant coach had found an unshaven, drunk, and fortunately clothed man in her bed. Then we found that the boys and girls had adjacent rooms in this fleabag place, so after a quick meeting we parents decided that we would keep our doors open at all times. As old Chicago wag Finley Peter Dunne once wrote as the sage Mr. Dooley, "Trust everybody, but cut the cards."

The weekend was Disney, Great Adventure, spring break, and the Final Four all in one. I think I made two dozen trips in my rental car the twenty-five minutes up and back through the mountains from the fleabag to the lake, and each one was packed with laughing kids. Athletically, it was beautiful as well. I didn't know that in crew, there was a national JV competition, but there was, and the Haddonfield JV four-girl boat won it. Ella's lightweight boat, mostly sophomores with one freshman and one junior, came in twelfth.

I came home on the bus, which was a riot of bad teenage movie videos, stops at fast food stands, and cacophonous singing.

It should have been, like in *Casablanca*, the beginning of a beautiful friendship.

Sue and I both work at home in offices that were probably bedrooms for more than a hundred years before we bought this rambling house. Given today's technology, sometimes we e-mail each other and other times we phone, even though Sue's office is on the third floor, just atop mine. We both have a habit of watching CNBC, so those e-mails and phone calls often are just about some flip remark made by one of our favorite anchors or how dismal or wonderful the stock market is that day.

Occasionally, I break from work and trundle upstairs for a visit. This one September afternoon I did so as Sue put on her headphones and, coincidentally, her phone rang.

She gave a little "Un-huh" to the caller at first and then lit out with a mighty "Yahoo" and performed a huge triple fist-pump. She then ripped off her headphones and threw them up in glee, something I had never seen her do.

"Ella just called from the team bus," she said, almost out of breath. "Jeff made her captain with Vera."

It may be one of those chicken-and-egg arguments: Which came first, the good Haddonfield tennis players or Jeff Holman to coach them? Each year, astoundingly, sixty or so girls in the fall and a like number of boys in the spring play on Holman's teams, which means that about one in every five or six kids at Haddonfield High gets to play some version of high school tennis each year.

Holman is a longtime teacher and now counselor at the high school who himself graduated from the high school and then Princeton University, about forty-five minutes up the road. He is also the winningest high school tennis coach in U.S. history. By the time Sylvia is a senior on the team, he may well have his thousandth girls' tennis win and will be in the nine hundreds with boys. The teams have won innumerable Group II (lower midsized schools) South Jersey and state championships. There are so many good players that in many years the third team at Haddonfield would be the third best team in the Colonial Conference, and almost always the second team could defeat nearly any team in South Jersey.

So you might expect Holman to be some regal martinet with myriad assistants doing his bidding. In fact, he's not.

When the sticky berries from the trees surrounding the five lone municipal courts at Centennial Field drop and gum them up from baseline to baseline, it is Holman, usually alone, out there sweeping and scraping them up. His clipboard, always in hand during matches, is full of results and matrices indicating which kids are playing whom. Though only the top three singles and two doubles matches count for score, at least a dozen other kids and often twice that many get some action each match. Holman finds extra courts for the thirty or so kids who don't travel as part of the varsity to play in a sort of intramural league. He drives the school bus to away matches and is often at the school late at night, figuring out who will play whom the next day and writing the zillions of college and other recommendations he is asked for as a counselor.

He is self-effacing and laconic and always asks, as the players go off the court, "Did you have a good time?"—which the girls, giggling, emblazoned on the shirts they made at one of their many T-shirt parties. The team rarely practices, since Holman schedules matches practically every day. He is the perennial head of the South Jersey Tennis Coaches Association and pretty much makes up one sort of tournament or other nearly every weekend. In winters, he is the scoreboard operator for all home basketball games, boys' or girls'. It would not surprise me if he pointed the bricks and cleaned out the gutters at the school in the summer.

One Friday night at about 10 P.M. when she was a freshman, Ella got a call from Jeff asking softly, as if he might be waking the family up with his voice on the phone, whether she would like to play in the Camden County Doubles Championships the next day. This was one of those quasi-made-up tournaments, just so every kid gets a chance in the sunshine. Ella and her doubles partner, Katie, were probably eighth or ninth best on the team, but because of Holman's nature, generosity, and maybe compulsiveness, they were going to play in a "championship."

So when he made Ella a captain it was, at once, both a surprise and typical. Ella had progressed apace as a tennis player from that freshman year, but there was never any way she was going to be in the vaunted top seven, or maybe even in the next seven. Her friend Vera, who lived across the street, was clearly the best senior player and could have beaten Ella soundly. Ella had hung in there and, in an underclass-heavy team, one that had won the state Group II championship the year before with only one senior among the top kids, was going to be the second-best senior.

Her second-teamness made becoming a captain even more of an honor. Most high school sports captains, particularly girls, are the best players, primarily seniors, on the team. Sometimes, they even eschew seniors when the juniors are the better players. Choosing Ella, especially her being so far down in the lineup, meant she had to have moxie and personality far beyond what even I thought. The year before, she had been a JV basketball captain, and all that coxswaining, with its imperious commands on both land and river, was at least some evidence that somewhere on those fields, she was doing something worthwhile in those leadership roles.

Meanwhile, Sylvia seemed to wend her way toward tennis as well. She had taken up goalkeeping in soccer in sixth grade and seemed to like the game enough. She did well in the high school coach's middle school camp, but then she played in West Deptford, a town 15 miles down the road, and didn't get any better.

When Sylvia got to seventh grade, though, Norm Hinsey, whose daughter Vera would be co-captain of the tennis team with Ella their senior year, told me about what he called "secret tennis." His son, Derek, a year older than Sylvia, went to a local indoor tennis center on Friday nights and, with other middle school kids, got free instruction from Coach Holman and his assistants.

Secret tennis was yet another of Holman's acts of goodwill. As if he didn't have enough to do, he and his assistants donated their time those winter Friday nights to any middle school kid who wanted to join in, so Sylvia happily did—maybe only to get out of the house and away from me grousing about what inane TV shows she would watch, zombie-like, all night.

After that, Norm, who was actually a tennis partner of mine, told me about super-secret tennis, a further permutation in which the coaches, still on their own time, took some of the better middle schoolers on Saturday nights and had them play matches against other towns. I really thought he was kidding, since I thought I was pretty plugged into the sports scene in town and had never heard of anything like this.

That was until one of the assistant coaches saw me at one of Ella's basketball games and asked me whether Sylvia would like to play Saturday nights. Sylvia was beside me, and when the coach left, I grabbed her cell phone and immediately dialed Norm.

"Sylvia is going to be in super-secret tennis," I whispered, as if George Bush had just told us she would be inducted into Skull and Bones, the super-secret society at Yale he belonged to as an undergraduate. "What's next? Special handshakes? Sheep's blood on the doorpost?"

In truth, Sylvia barely scraped by in super-secret tennis. Her best move, as I told her, was getting on a mixed doubles team with an old kindergarten classmate who could whack the fur off the ball. Her next best move was learning the finger-point upward, which means the opponent's shot had gone out of bounds.

Still, she was under Coach Holman's spell, and the soccer demons had been cast aside. Her West Deptford team that eighth-grade year had some really fun girls, but few of them were any good at soccer. The team limped through the spring season, not just losing every game but getting all of one goal in doing so—and that was by a guest player in the first game. The coach was a lovely man, though, patient and forgiving. He put them in a Memorial Day tournament and asked Sylvia whether she wanted to bring a couple of Haddonfield friends down to play.

Sure enough, the team, with Sylvia's two ringers, won two of three games and got nifty trophies for their final efforts. West Deptford had a soccer banquet at one of those humongous catering houses that lasted about three and a half hours, with every kid in every age group getting some kind of kudos from a coach. Sylvia came home with a trophy about 3 feet high for being the most cooperative kid, or something like that.

"Don't worry, Dad, I'm playing tennis," she said as we left the catering joint with that and at least three other trophies and certificates.

With that, the shackles of youth soccer had left us. No more A, B, or 78-mile trips to play "equal" opponents. It was as liberating as a gallon of Alka Seltzer, as cathartic as an enema.

One Friday evening in the spring of Ella's sophomore year in high school, I had to do an errand in Philadelphia and asked her to come for company, which she didn't mind. As we were heading out of town back toward home, about 7 P.M., she said, "I don't know who to call. Don't know what to do tonight."

I suggested calling one of her basketball teammates, the one who had hosted an end-of-the-season sleepover the weekend before.

"Couldn't do that," Ella answered immediately, as if I had suggested calling, say, Chelsea Clinton, whom she had once met when we lived at Stanford for a year.

"Why not?" I asked, knowing well that I was probably a fool for asking.

"Basketball season's over," she said. "Can't call now."

In fact, this was not such a bad thing. As seasons changed for the Strauss girls, friendships could, too. In a manic and multifaceted household, the transitions kept the girls fresh.

I think the sports kept them organized at school, too. The period of freshman year when Sylvia quit basketball to be manager was her worst scholastically. She often came home and just vegetated in front of the TV set. She was always an A-plus kind of student, so the A-minus weeks weren't a disaster, but I was happy when lacrosse season started; even with less time, homework went first.

The girls' social lives never seemed to suffer either. I couldn't say which clique or group was the most popular, but I never thought the girls foundered in that regard. At least in Haddonfield, the jock girls seemed to be those in the vanguard in everything. This became another reason to be in sports.

Our family vice, and the place where the girls seemed as joyous as I to be different, was our goofball traveling. Since I never went anywhere as a kid except from New York to Washington—my parents weren't poor, just not the traveling type—I wanted to go everywhere once I realized I could. I had been only to the three North American countries until I was twenty-nine and my father died abruptly. An old girlfriend said she was going to Europe for a month, so I tagged along.

Thirty years onward, I have been to all fifty states and nearly a hundred countries. I have dragged the girls to lunch in Slovakia and snacks in Slovenia. Ella and I have camped through Africa twice, and Sylvia and I took a cab to Albania, since it was only a few miles from where we were staying in Macedonia, as if that were the normal place a thirteen-year-old would want to go. Ella said she wanted to go to fifty countries by the time she was in college and was two short the summer before senior year in high school. Sue and I had wanted to go to the Amazon, so I discovered a town, Letitia, Colombia, that was on the Amazon and right next to both Peru and Brazil—so close I walked to Brazil for breakfast one day.

So the Strauss girls have taken up not only the sports cudgel of the family but also the oddball traveling one. I believe each plays off the other; in each, participation with gusto is far more important than winning.

"Hello, Strauss Family," went the cheery voice of my friend Mike on the phone message tape. Like me, Mike was an inveterate reader of the minuscule agate type of statistics in the high school sports pages of the local newspapers.

It was a welcoming phone call to the honor roll of high school athletics. Mike's kids were star runners, so he was a veteran of the agate glory. The night before, Haddonfield's girls' basketball team had annihilated Paulsboro, a local working-class school more known for its wrestling teams, which won some ungodly number, like two dozen, state championships in a row but was woeful in things like girls' basketball. The score was 68–35, but down there in the agate, past the girls with double figures, and even those who had seven or eight, was "Ella Strauss—3."

There were probably three hundred names in agate type in the newspaper that morning, but Mike knew that his mention of it to me on that message tape would be like, say, President Clinton calling to remember my birthday or Jennifer Aniston phoning me personally to come over and watch an episode of *Friends*.

Every so often, one of Sue's Saturday morning coffee-klatch buddies, Bob Parsons, videotapes games of various sorts and will make a DVD for a nominal sum. The day after the Paulsboro game, Sue discovered that Bob had been taping as Ella, who was put in during the second period to spell the best athlete in her class, Emily Grabiak, at point guard, zipped up the court after a Paulsboro basket. The captain and best player on the team, Annie Maloney, started bringing the ball up but soon found that no Paulsboro girl had taken notice of the five-foot squirt who had jetted into the left-hand corner.

Zip went Annie's pass to Ella. Swish went Ella's long three-pointer.

"Call Bob. Get that DVD," demanded Sue. "We may never see its like again."

Three days later, Bob came to the front door, I handed him a $10 bill, and he handed me the DVD as if it were contraband headed toward the Spanish Front. I popped it into the player and fast-forwarded it to The Shot. Ella was not at home, but

I screeched for Sue to come watch. The whole sequence took, at most, seven seconds, but Sue said, "Best ten bucks you have ever spent."

As I wrote this, three years later, I went across the room to the cabinet below that same DVD player. The disc is still in its holder, still reading "Haddonfield 68, Girls' Basketball, 1-15-2008, Paulsboro 35." It is still cued up to The Shot. Ella never did know we bought it.

Unfortunately, it was the only three-pointer of her varsity career.

In fact, the only other video we have of Ella playing for Haddonfield was the last game she ever played on JV. I was never one to use the video camera. I liked watching live and was not particularly adept with such things.

Ella's varsity stints were never all that long, and it was always unclear when they would come. I loved watching the games, though, and many days during her junior year would start with me at about 3:45 watching Sylvia's middle school game, then going to the JV game, home or away, at about 5:30 and staying for the varsity game at 7. It was particularly nutty, since Ella would normally play parts of three quarters of the JV game and be "saved" for varsity—kids are allowed to play parts of five quarters a night in New Jersey—which meant she would get in at the end if the team was up or down by a lot.

That was hardly a video camera type of thing.

Yet this last game against Overbrook, the JV coach had told me that he was going to play Ella as much as she was able. He had loved having her, he said, and she had never given him a moment's trouble. Though Overbrook was not a particular draw, it would be the last home game, and Ella, like the rest of the varsity players, would be giving a rose to her mom between games, as Haddonfield tradition dictated.

So this time, I charged up the old video camera that probably had been sitting in the closet since Ella's and my camping trip to Uganda five years before and took a seat in the back frosty row of the old gym, out of the way of the two dozen or so other folks, primarily parents, coming out for the JV game.

I have not replayed the tape and only hope to save it for the grandchildren. Like the Battle of Britain for the Royal Air Force, this was Ella's finest hour. It was JV against mediocre competition, but the little buzzsaw had thirteen points, with a three-pointer, and went six for eight from the foul line. She had three assists, three rebounds, and an amazing nine steals. What Sue loved best was the play where Ella planted herself in the lane and took a big, fat charge from a muscular Overbrook girl at least a foot taller and certainly 50 pounds heavier.

I packed the video camera away slowly as the between-games ceremony started. By the time I got down to the floor, Sue had the rose in her hand, but she also had both of her arms wrapped around Ella, who was bawling like I hadn't seen her do since, I guess, kindergarten.

There were lots of folks around, especially other parents and players, but Ella looked my way in mid-bawl and waved me away with several swift, abrupt flings of her arm.

The basketball cycle that had begun with those first three layups on Rich Edwards's town league team had wound up in that Overbrook JV game toward midnight, and she was not going to let me find a glass slipper to stop it.

Whoa, There's a Mom Here, Too

If my wife is right, we met at a Halloween party in 1981, given by a mutual friend at his house along the Hudson River, overlooking the Tappan Zee Bridge. I had recently started working at *Sports Illustrated*, so I was a bit giddy, having landed a job at the place where I dreamed of being since kindergarten.

I was wearing the orange overalls I had gotten when in the cast of *Peter Pan* my junior year at Carleton College. I appropriately played one of the Lost Boys, Nibs. I was thirty by the time I reached that party and was still a bit lost, though orange did seem the right color for Halloween. On one of the straps of the overalls I had stapled a paper cutout circle, and on that circle was an ink-stamped visage of Tom Haller, the old San Francisco Giants catcher. My *Sports Illustrated* colleague Franz Lidz had an odd collection of rubber stamps he kept in his drawer at the office, and one of them was of Haller, who probably would not have known how he got on a rubber stamp. Franz has a somewhat absurdist sense of humor; for instance, he named his daughters Gogo, after the nickname of one of the main characters in Samuel Beckett's landmark absurdist play *Waiting for Godot*, and Daisy Daisy. When Sue was pregnant with

Sylvia, we were testing out names, and we told Franz that since we had Ella, we were thinking of Aretha as a complementary second-child's name. "Nah, too silly," he told us. Given who shot us down on that, we stuck with Sylvia.

Anyhow, that night, he convinced me I should have the mark of Tom Haller on me since it was "Haller-ween."

I went with it, but I do not think it initially attracted Sue, sporting though it was. I doubt she had ever heard of Tom Haller, and I am certain she thought wearing orange overalls to a New York party absurd—and not in the more positive Samuel Beckett sense.

We met for certain a few years later, after I had left *Sports Illustrated*. She had come to Philadelphia for a job interview, and we met through a mutual friend, but then Sue took a job at the *Baltimore Evening Sun*, and I countered that, leaving my TV producing job to be a sports columnist for a set of suburban Philadelphia newspapers. They sent me to all the big events: the World Series, the Super Bowl, U.S. Open golf, Triple Crown horse races, and the run of Philadelphia pro and college team games.

Sue could not have cared less about sports, which, in my contrarian view, was just about right. Traveling constantly in the sports world, I had had enough of it and its players and commentators by the time Sue and I met. Oh, she liked the sidelines of sports; for instance, the infield Preakness party is basically a drunken spring fiesta interrupted rather unnecessarily by a two-and-a-half-minute gallop. At the Preakness parties, they make a drink called the Black-Eyed Susan, named after the Maryland state flower, and I know she liked that when we went. I think she may have even liked me.

She ended up having two daughters with me, whom I know she likes just fine.

When Sue resigned from the *Philadelphia Inquirer* in 2001 after fifteen years there, I picked her up from work and drove her home. The girls were then ten and seven and already well into their sporting times. On the porch, I had set up two gray cloth folding "soccer" chairs, each with a sizable cup holder on the right armrest. Sue was not exactly retiring, but since I had made it as a freelance writer, she was going to give it a try, too. Part of the deal was that she was going to get interested in the girls' budding athletic careers and become, at least for a trial run, a soccer mom, so she definitely needed the right equipment right there on the porch.

During the 1996 presidential race, conventional wisdom had it that the deciding voter type between Republican Robert Dole and Democrat Bill Clinton would be suburban white women. "The working soccer mom is the swing voter of this election," Republican consultant Alex Castellanos proclaimed to the *Wall Street Journal.* Unfortunately, at that point the term "soccer mom" was pretty much a derogatory appellation, popular mostly from a 1991 case in which an apparently world-wearied California mother drove to lots of kid sporting events. The sentiment is that that drove her nuts, since she shot her two daughters and then turned the gun, unsuccessfully, on herself.

Sue had never described herself much as an athlete, but one day soon after her entry into soccer momdom, the girls discovered in the attic their mom's varsity cheerleading trophy from Dearborn High School in that Michigan city, Ford Motor Company's headquarters, where she grew up. The girls and I immediately shined the brass figure on the trophy and put it up on the fireplace mantel. For a moment, at least, Sue reveled in the disclosure of her cheerleading past and tried a few rickety-racks and arm-and-leg twisting jumps. The girls, who had previously considered cheerleading at best a bother and certainly not a worthy athletic endeavor, in turn cheered, or heckled, Sue on. Having a soccer mom, they decided, was going to be fun.

It is on shifting sands that such hopes are born. The reality of being a soccer mom is that it requires a combination of providing transportation, schmoozing with other soccer moms, putting up with Dad's interest in his daughters' athletic endeavors, and, finally, being jeered by those daughters.

Part of the newfound mass entry of girls in sports over the last twenty years or so is that they routinely think their moms know nothing about anything that has a ball, stroke, or sneaker.

"That was a really good play," Sue might say innocuously to Ella or Sylvia after a game, to which the reply was almost invariably something like, "Ugh! It was miserable. What do you know?"

Had I said exactly the same thing about exactly the same play, they would probably have smiled, said a shy, "Thanks," and asked advice about how to improve it even more the next time.

It would have been a reverse *Rashomon*, in which the subject would see herself differently based on her observer. To a twenty-first-century girl jock, Mom cannot possibly know what she is talking about when it comes to sports, and Dad, even if you don't exactly agree with him, must know something about what he is saying. After all, Dad probably at least watched the sport, if not played it, as a kid. As much as we think we have progressed in gender equity, sex stereotyping is pretty much alive and well, and it can work to Mom's advantage sometimes. Would even the most liberated daughter allow Dad on a prom dress search? Listen to his opinion on eyeliner? Tolerate for a second his caustic commentary about *Real Housewives of New Jersey?*

This had to gall Sue, especially since we both grew up in politically conservative households and, despite that, became lifelong liberals. I hold on to a few guy things—I like to do the driving, for instance—but for the most part, we are rock-ribbed egalitarians, and we hoped that Ella and Sylvia would follow our lead.

After a time, though, it must have become too wearing on Sue, and she said, "Heck with it, I am going to cheer when I darned well feel like it." She has a marvelous fingers-in-the-mouth whoop-whistle, and she uses it at any game, good moments and bad, just like that. She quickly tries to learn the names of all the girls on all the teams, which I am dreadful at. Philadelphians tend to call everyone "Hon," even when they know their names. It is almost an honorific, or at least a term of respect, like "Ma'am," not a throwaway like "Hey, You."

Still, Sue cringed when I constantly yelled things like "Great pass, Hon," to Ella's or Sylvia's teammates. She thought it sort of creepy—a middle-aged man leeringly calling out sweetness to a preteen girl. I could not quite convince her that it was just part of my Philly-ness, but I had little choice, as the plethora of Alexises and Brookes and Emilys and Kyras just confused the heck out of me, especially since all of them seemed to have blond ponytails, skinny legs, and, for a time, braced teeth.

For the most part, despite the seeming ubiquity of the term "soccer mom," even girls' youth sports is Dad's World. Only three times on their dozens of youth sports teams did the girls have a mom as a coach or even an assistant. Only once, actually, was a mom a head coach, and even then, the mom did it only because no one else would step up that particular season. Dads then get other dads to be their assistants. Then more dads feel guilty and start doing the clock or manning a sideline. Soon it is a testosterone shell encasing a blond ponytail tadpole sea.

So it is no wonder that even our girls, who sincerely love their mother, gave Sue less than half a chance when it came to sports. Oh, occasionally they disparaged my knowledge, too ("So, Dad, how many lacrosse games did you play?" is a typical Sylvia response when I misinterpret some strategy in that most arcane of games), but normally they just completely shut down the conversation if Sue asked more than the score of the game.

I never perceived that to be a problem with my mom. I remember her doing only one sporting kind of thing with me, and then I think it happened only a couple of times. Mom was left-handed, and since I was right-handed, there were only right-handed baseball gloves around the house. But I have this vision of Mom, probably in one of her few idle moments, putting on my old Bobby Knoop model glove—Knoop (pronounced "keh-NOP") being a marginal infielder of the 1960s—backwards, splaying it on her right hand. I remember her being quite adept at fielding my usually errant throws.

I also remember my mom being at only one of my many sporting events. She and Dad came to only one Parents' Weekend when I was at Carleton—which is understandable since it was 1,200 or so miles northwest of Cherry Hill in Minnesota—but that just happened to be when I was playing rugby against the University of Minnesota. Other than that, neither she nor my father was ever at any of my high school club basketball or varsity track, cross-country, or tennis matches, my freshman basketball games, or any of my other rugby matches at Carleton. I can't say that she ever even watched me play Wiffle ball, wire ball, handball, touch football, or any of the other games we made up playing in the backyard or front driveway.

Sometimes, she told me stories about the Baron Dougherty, a Pennsylvania relative—the father of her cousin's husband—who ran a bookmaking, boxing, and wrestling business during her youth in the 1920s and the Depression in Chester, Pennsylvania, a tough burg both now and then. One time in her early teens when she was visiting, there was a big hubbub in the Baron's backyard, where he had a makeshift boxing ring. She went over to peer through a knothole, and there was a bare-chested Jack Dempsey, the world's heavyweight champ, beating up on some poor dope.

Though she didn't say much about sports to me, Mom knew I was hooked on them. When I was thirteen, the Phillies made a run at the pennant, and I got to listen to them on my Uncle Sid's recent bar mitzvah present to me: a rather large brown pseudo-leather-encased transistor radio that didn't have an automatic shutoff. I would fall asleep to Richie Ashburn and Byrum Saam announcing those summer games. The Phillies got ahead by six and a half games with twelve to play, seemingly an insurmountable lead. But this was the Phillies, and they lost the next ten games. My mother would leave me a note of what happened at the end of each game to which I fell asleep. It was a tragedy in missives, endearing nonetheless.

Moms, then, weren't objects of disdain. We just didn't expect them to do anything at all. Mostly, they didn't even drive us to games or practices. Except once, at least as I remember.

In high school, a bunch of us were basketball junkies. We wouldn't miss an opportunity to play ball. Four of us especially—Irish Jack Deeney; Paul Richards, who moved from Tennessee with his hound-dog look and thick accent, in ninth grade; my second-grade buddy Gary Popowcer; and I—played endless two-on-two games, even though I was never up to their skill level. There was an old indoor ice rink near Paul's house, which was about 2 miles from the rest of ours, that kept two movable fiberglass backboard hoops in a storage area. Once a year, apparently, some lesser version of the Harlem

Globetrotters came to town. They would roll out these hoops, and the jokester ballplayers would play their circus-like game on the cement surface below the ice.

Paul had worked in the concession stand for a hockey game at the rink—first named the Ice House and then the Cherry Hill Arena—and discovered the hoops in storage, with just enough room in front of one to play a half-court game. The next day, we went over there and found an open window. We crawled in and were able to play for at least an hour before some employee shooed us away. Still, we were sure we could do this forever: basketball Nirvana.

The next weekend, we had my mother drive us to the arena, saying we were going ice skating. Mysteriously, though, we were carrying a basketball with us. She dropped us off, and we quickly made our way around back to that still-open window. As the first of us shimmied up to crawl in, we heard a car coming around.

"Uh, hi, Mrs. Strauss," Jack said in his usual Eddie-Haskell-please-the-parents voice. (Eddie was a seminal sitcom character, older brother Wally's friend on *Leave It to Beaver*, who always spoke politely to parents to their faces, then busted them an insult after they left.) "Just looking for a basketball hoop."

My mother looked cross for a moment but then pulled the car's hood up near the window. She motioned to us to get on. One by one, we got up on the hood and snuggled through that window, and then she drove off, an unindicted co-conspirator for our teenaged sporting Jones.

Sue was a bit more skeptical about the character-building nature of sports than I. Whenever one of the girls had a bad reaction to a game, an injury, or a demotion to second string or, even more sadly, the B team, she would tell them that Model U.N. would be a better fit. Though the girls were world travelers and would clearly know more about, say, the West Bank than any Model U.N. kid, they would only grunt when Sue brought such things up. Did Model U.N.-sters wear nifty sweatshirts? What about Bulldawg socks or, better, bruises of honor? The intoned phrase "Model U.N." soon became better than any antiseptic or analgesic at curing a sporting slight or injury.

Sue did revel in the sidelights of the girls' sports, if not the substance. When Ella first got on the purple squad in her five-year-olds soccer team, Sue took her to the first practice. Down the sidelines, she saw a hulking tall figure, almost an apparition from her youth. It was Marty Szuba, the best swimmer in Michigan her senior year in high school, a seemingly impossible connection from 600 miles away and twenty years in the past. Marty's son was a purple, too, so fate had connected.

"This sports thing may not be as bad as I thought," Sue told me. Marty had been the star of stars: smart, good-looking, and talented. Maybe Ella would get something out of it. Unfortunately, within a couple of years Marty got cancer and died quickly. In some ways, from my perspective, Sue never caught up from that. The one thing in Ella's sporting life that was hers, not mine, was lost.

Youth sports seemed more of a tension than a joy. Sue was the Girl Scout leader, and each date for a weekend campout seemed thwarted by the great devil soccer. One year, an assistant basketball coach bought all the girls on Sylvia's team special socks. Since, as the cliché goes, every clothes washing yields an odd number of socks, Sue told me years later that she worried that the wash would end with only one of the special socks out of the dryer, and Sylvia would be ostracized or, worse, robbed of playing time in the next game, so she washed the socks separately and line-dried them each time. Ella's bat mitzvah fell on the day of a youth soccer game, so many of the girls she invited stayed for only an hour of the party, changing from dresses to shin pads in the synagogue powder room.

Still, there were some daughter–mommy moments. When Ella marched onto the floor at the start of her first middle school basketball game, she motioned to me to have Mommy turn her way. Looking up at her, only her, up the flight of stands, Ella mouthed silently, with a huge teeth-braced grin, "I'm starting."

I can only imagine that the night before, Ella had had a crisis of confidence only a rubdown from Mommy could cure—a Don't Worry, You're Great session Sue gave, even in the face of a chance to promote Model U.N.

The year the girls were on the varsity tennis team together, Sue pretty much stayed away. Tennis was generally too boring to watch, and if she had to pick watching one over the other, were they not playing on nearby courts, that would ruin things all the more.

One weekend match, though, the girls must have told their coach, the always-accommodating Jeff Holman, that their mom was going to show up. They meant little by this, just idle conversation, no doubt.

Jeff took it as a signal. For the first time, he had them listed as doubles partners. Ella was usually farther up the tennis food chain than Sylvia, being better and being team co-captain as well. What we never realized was that this also kept them from ever having to play with or even near each other.

This particular Saturday, though, at Eastern High School, the girls got to play together in front of Mom. We brought both the video and still cameras.

What we didn't bring that we should have was a federal mediator. None of us knew that they couldn't stand playing together, and it was only because they adored Jeff Holman that they would deign to do it.

The match was akin to the famous U.S.S.R.–Hungary water polo game at the 1956 Olympics. That took place soon after the Soviets mowed down the Hungarian rebels trying to convert their country to a democracy. The pool where the game was played was the scene of a bloody battle, each side taking every opportunity to kick and maul someone on the other team.

The Strauss girls were on the same team this time around, but I feared bloodshed after the first few practice swings. I had rarely seen their faces so twisted and nasty looking. Apparently, they were holding everything in, not for Sue's sake, I am sure, but for Coach Holman's. Since it was fifth or sixth doubles, the score wouldn't matter, but they should have been clear favorites. They lost in straight sets and then walked off in different directions.

We skipped the video, and Sue skipped most of the rest of tennis season.

Sue's biggest sporting effort was the book she wrote with her friend Jennifer Lin, *Sole Sisters*, inspirational stories about women who found strength running with their compadres. Sue was not all that much of a runner herself. She had broken both of her ankles at one time or another and always feared they might refracture if she put too much stress on them. She does a lot of walking, especially with friends she likes to coffee-down and chat with while the pounds, hopefully, slide away.

She had hoped, too, that the girls would run sometime during school, which would inspire her to run more herself. It didn't happen while they were still girls, but you never know. Maybe that will be the adult game plan: Daddy's Little Goalie and her sister will become Mommy's Gabby Running Partners, and that will be just fine, just fine indeed.

Intensity and the Nonsports Experience
Competitiveness Doesn't Stop Off the Court Either

There is little question that the competition on the field, the courts, and the water made Ella and Sylvia competitive in their other endeavors. In the broader definition, sports competitiveness wafted into games. Rules for cards and Monopoly and shuffleboard and checkers would get modified depending on what aspect of the strategy they were good at—and if I were playing, whatever I seemed not to want. For instance, allowable words in Scrabble tended to include preteen girl lingo and exclude obscure "adult" formations.

Collingswood, the rival town 2 miles down Haddon Avenue, has been gussying up its main drags of late, restaurants of all sorts and prices springing up despite the town's prohibition against liquor licenses.

Late in her high school senior year, Ella discovered the Monday night Quiz Nights at the Pop Shop, the updated-old-time ice cream joint in the middle of the Haddon Avenue restaurant district. Collingswood has successfully marketed itself to young adult singles, straight and gay, with cheap prices and a train station four stops into Philly, so Quiz Night, even without a bar, attracts a crowd as diverse as it gets in the suburbs.

Ella and her friends, plus Sylvia and I, became regulars as The WestEnders, a play on the name of the BBC TV show *EastEnders* and our home address on West End Avenue. We bonded with the other regulars, like the Chocoholics and Werewolf Bar Mitzvah and Teachers Against Christie, Chris Christie being the New Jersey governor who cut education funding.

Our goal was to win the contest but win honorably. Our problem was that we were covered young, with Ella, Sylvia, and the high school crowd, and old, with me and sometimes another parent. Yet the quizzes were definitely geared to the rest of the crowd in their twenties and thirties. We were bang-up on categories like nursery rhymes and American history but woefully short when it came to *Top Gun* and Robert Downey Jr.

Still, we had our moments. One wonderful one was when Sylvia grabbed the shard of paper we were using as an answer sheet during a tie-breaker in the fifth-grade science category. It was that whole kingdom, phylum, and order list even the older high school kids had long forgotten. She won us a $15 second-place gift certificate all on her own.

Our moment in the sun was the Monday of Memorial Day weekend. We knew some of the teams would still be out lollygagging at the shore or barbecuing or just assuming Quiz Night would be off, but The WestEnders had business to do.

We were looking unusually good going into the final round, which is much like *Jeopardy!* in that you bet whatever part of your points you want on the category and then answer one last question. What we did not need was a category like, say, *One Day at a Time*, the mid-old TV show, which would definitely not fit in with our geriatric–teen axis.

When Mr. Know-It-All, the droll and poker-faced quizmaster, announced that the final round would be world geography, Ella and I went practically into apoplexy. Could there have been anything more Straussian, father and daughter, than that?

We handed in our final bet, which was everything we had. Actually, we always bet everything on the final answer, as does any self-respecting Pop Shop Quiz Night regular team. The whole point is that we believe we are at least junior Know-It-Alls. Winning because you bet nothing and everyone else strove for glory on the final answer, falling short by not knowing the answer, was without honor—a black mark like hitting home runs while taking steroids, or some near-equivalent.

Then the fear went through Ella and me. The pressure was on. Sometimes, in competition, with the signs all pointing your way, there might be only a downside risk. The girls had long ago learned from sports that the team you feel can't beat you is just the team that will find a way to do so. One of their favorite movies was *Guys and Dolls*. In a famous scene—one that I pointed out to them as advice so many times, their eyes would roll inward at the mere thought of it—Sky Masterson, played by Marlon Brando, refuses a sucker bet offered by Nathan Detroit, played by Frank Sinatra, with the following lines:

"When I was a young man about to go out in the world, my father says to me a very valuable thing. 'Son,' the old guy says, 'one of these days in your travels a guy is going to come to you with a brand new deck of cards and offer to bet you that he can make the Jack of Spades jump out of the deck and squirt cider in your ear. But Son, do not bet this man, for as sure as you are standing there, you are going to wind up with an ear full of cider.'"

We waited on the question, which was going to be multiple choice. There it was, like a hanging curve: "What is the capital of Albania?" Though we had not gotten to Tirana, Sylvia and I had only recently been to Albania, perhaps the only people in Collingswood at that moment, including those hip and happening thirty-year-olds, who had ever been to that most backward of European countries.

"Wait," Ella warned. "Are you sure? Are you really sure? There's no trick?"

Actually, the only trick was that some Werewolf Bar Mitzvah-ite or Chocoholic might guess right. If it were a straight answer, no multiple choice, I would have been more confident.

"No, Ella. I might not be able to cox a boat, but you will have to go with me here," I said.

Sure enough, after the tabulations, the WestEnders won our first Pop Shop Quiz Night crown. Ella's friend Wyatt demanded that our cute waitress be in our winners' photo with us, and our team name went up on the chalkboard facing out the window for all to see. This time, it was a $25 gift certificate.

More importantly, though, it was daddy–daughter pride in our best-category-for-us victory together.

I have to admit that if I had to choose something the girls would be really marvelous at, it would have been music. Early on, though, I knew I was not going to win that one.

When we lived in married student housing at Stanford during Sue's fellowship, there was just enough room along one wall of the living room for a narrow upright piano, so I rented one from the university. With my small cache of mostly Sinatraesque or early rock music, I banged on it a few hours a week, while my neighbors rolled their eyes skyward and tolerated the discord.

At some point, Ella, in kindergarten but no doubt sensing that she could be better than Dad in about a half dozen shots at the keyboard, asked for lessons. We found a student to give her some, and when Ella did "Claire de Lune" perfectly by the third lesson, I was already mentally booking us with dual pianos, à la Ferrante and Teicher, in smoky clubs from the Bowery to Nob Hill.

Back in Haddonfield in second grade, she chose the cello as her grade school stringed instrument in typical Straussian contrarianism: Few else wanted to play it. Sylvia was even more so, selecting the viola because no one else wanted to play that. When nonstringed instruments were on offer in the school, Ella went for the clarinet and lasted, warily, until middle school, then begged off. The best horn player in the school, a shy kid, pleaded with her to stick with it, that she was the best clarinet player in the school and that the band truly needed her.

This was indeed the case. It is not that the Marching Colonials, the Haddonfield High School marching band, is full of sad-sack players. It is just that the school is so sports obsessed, nearly everyone who could ever play a trumpet or bang a marimba plays field hockey or soccer or football, or rows or runs or is in off-season training. I think I once counted seventeen Marching Colonials at halftime of a Friday night tussle, even when the football team was in its era of 3–6 seasons.

Ella slowly opted out, sticking with piano lessons for a little while, then fading to black. Sylvia was both more competitive and defiant. She rarely missed a lesson, even doing some supplements, on the clarinet through seventh grade, but she rarely practiced at home. Still, the urge to win got her into the South Jersey All-Star Orchestra a year early.

Just as in her Tri-County diving saga, once she had made it, Sylvia was through. Like a check mark on the wall, or the climactic moments of "Stars and Stripes Forever," this, too, was the end note. The day when "8th Grade Band" disappeared abruptly from her schedule on the school Web site severed my daughters from music. Oh, once in a while, Sylvia will come into my office and bang a few notes on the vibraphone I keep there, and at parties Ella still plays "Heart and Soul," but the Music Mountain, in their version, got climbed early and conquered, and that was that.

The girls also seemed to love the competition of the ballot box. Ella early on was the liberal lone wolf in a sea of elementary school conservatives. For its first three centuries or so, Haddonfield never elected anyone of the Democratic persuasion. Finally, just before we moved there in 1989, Jack Tarditi, the first Democrat ever to serve on the Board of Commissioners, became mayor.

Soon after we moved in, a neighbor invited us to a party and Jack was there. He was holding court between the crudités and the Diet Coke station, so I sidled up to meet him. I asked this inane question:

"So in Haddonfield, is it the strong mayor system or the weak mayor system?" Showing high school civics class knowledge is about as bottom-scraping as it gets in trying to ingratiate yourself in a new town, but it was what came front and center at the moment.

Fortunately, Jack is voluble and clever.

"In Haddonfield," he said, volume turned up as always, "it is the loud mayor system."

Jack keeps that volume up with the energy of a cheetah on caffeine. His weekend bicycle rides on the island where we go to the beach often correspond to my early morning Stone Harbor basketball games. As he rides by leisurely with friends and I am busting a gut trying to keep up with ballplayers half and sometimes a quarter of my age, he will always yell out, "Strauss, get moving," and squeeze his "ah-oo-gah" horn at me.

He got me in an early morning tennis group for a time that seemed to be more of a smoke-filled-room arrangement. Everyone there had a title. Even after he stopped being mayor, Jack was always addressed in this group as "Mayor." A former county sheriff there was still "Sheriff," and deposed pols were still "Senator" or "Councilman." Every so often, time would be called and business would be discussed on the sidelines. Since most of the group was Italian or Hispanic, there were mandatory hugs going on and off the court. Jews, I have to say, don't do much of the showman ballyard celebrating. After a zillion years, I still don't know whether I should be high fiving, fist bumping, or merely hand shaking with my compadres after a win or good play. I don't think I have ever chest bumped or soul shaked. The girls, too, are similarly shake-averse. Girls' sports these days—particularly in basketball, where individuals are announced—put one nonstarter on the court at the end of a corridor of subs, which the starters go through as they are announced. That lone girl's job is to do the particular shake or series of shakes or bumps the starter desires. It is a fun bit of choreography, but Ella and Sylvia never really warmed to it, their small bit of conservativeness coming to the fore.

I think it was Jack's volubility that got Ella interested in politics. Soon after she was born, he asked me to help out, as a volunteer, figuring out how to publicize the borough's doings. I brought Ella to meetings in a backpack, and she slept through many of them. Still, she got proper coos and chin-chuckles from every politician who came through, including, once, Bill Clinton as he was campaigning in the area for his first presidential term.

So when it came time to run for middle school office, Ella was ready. Not for a moment did she think of anything but president, though. Her scrappiness on the field and court made her goal an all-or-nothing one. Sure enough, with a Tippecanoe-like slogan, "Put Strauss in the House," she won her first election. She tried to capitalize and do it again freshman year in high school, but "Put Strauss Back in the House" was not as effective. The election was the day of her birthday party, and she lost by a slim margin to one of her best friends. It was a sort of intimate gathering, in the tatami room, cross-legged on the bamboo, of her favorite Japanese restaurant. I can't imagine even the cheerful Ronald Reagan and Walter Mondale sharing a meal after a presidential election, but the triumphant boy and the second-place Ella snarfed sushi and smiled cheek-to-cheek together.

One insight into the character of a sports participant is seeing what she is like as a sports fan. One of my favorite photographs of Ella is from the late spring of 2001. It was at the fifth and final game of NBA championships, and she is sitting there at the end of the game with one of the saddest nine-year-old-girl faces imaginable. On her right hand is one of those massive foam up-pointing fingers. Her face is painted with some red, white, and blue number indicating fast loyalty to the Philadelphia 76ers. Other detritus from the game surrounds her, and the seats are quickly emptying behind her. The Sixers had just been beaten, four games to one, by the vastly superior Los Angeles Lakers, and to a preadolescent fan, there is nothing more disappointing than the last game.

I believed that part of my responsibility as a valuable sports dad was teaching the girls how to be Philadelphia sports fans. People not from Philadelphia reading the last sentence will be growling that to put any version of "responsible" and

"Philadelphia sports fans" together is promoting a bigger oxymoron than "military intelligence" or "fine British cuisine."

Philadelphia sports fans have a reputation for being, at best, louts. At the first home game of the 2001 series between the Sixers and the Lakers, for instance, the halftime entertainment was Destiny's Child, hot even then before its lead singer, Beyoncé, went off on her own to worldwide acclaim.

The NBA, trying to be ecumenical, dressed one of Beyoncé's cohorts in a Sixers jersey and the other in a neutral NBA one. Beyoncé, though, came out in Lakers purple and gold. She was smiling and jangling and in good voice, but once the Philadelphia crowd caught a glimpse of her shirt, they stepped back from their halftime cheesesteaks and beers and let out a sonorous "Booooooooooo" that drowned out the young ladies' tones. Beyoncé, flustered and humiliated, started crying and left center court.

Halfway through that season, Ella saw during a telecast we were watching that the Sixers, well into first place in the NBA's Eastern Conference, had rest-of-the-season tickets left, with first dibs on playoff seats. She put on those moony eyes and the burgeoning lower lip. I went to the checkbook like a salmon to the hatchery.

By the Beyoncé game, she was a veteran of Sixers marketing mastery. Each playoff game, the team put on a fair outside the arena and in the hallways inside. When they played the Indiana Pacers in the opening round, for instance, fans could take a small sledge hammer, for a buck or two for charity, and take a swing at an old Pacer coupe. There would be jazz bands and dunk tanks and souvenir stands and huge cards to sign to send well wishes to star Allen Iverson and the rest of the team. Inside was free face painting for kids and drawings for paraphernalialike an Eric Snow Globe, with a replica of Snow, Iverson's backcourt mate, dribbling inside a plastic dome.

I gave up my seat for one of the playoff games so that Ella could show Sue the fiesta from her eyes. I think they headed to the game two hours early, but in any case, it was early enough to get there and see several players emerge from their Escalades and Jeeps on the team parking plaza below the party area. Ella pointed out just the right place to sign the celebratory card and chose the proper face painter for maximum cheek coverage.

The Sixers marketing guy, Dave Coskey, managed to come up with unusual halftime acts all through the season, and Ella had seen contortionists and plate spinners and Frisbee-catching dogs and acrobats of all sorts. As with cheerleaders, she was particularly disdainful of the intrusion of the Sixers Dance Team, each dancer's cleavage having the ability, I believe, to balance several basketballs from stem to stern.

"What use do they have?" she would say with an angry wag of her head each time the two dozen or so would prance onto the floor, followed by whoops and drools from a sizable cadre of the male Sixers faithful. "At least cheerleaders have some use. At least body-benders fill up halftime. Get the game going."

We kept those season tickets for the next two years, despite the Sixers' fading fates in those seasons. The seats were nothing glorious. It was the first row above the handicapped seats in the third deck in a corner at $21 a pop. We got to know the people around us and got particularly fond of the guys to our left. One had played ball at Drexel University with two other guys I knew back in the late 1970s. The other was his almost mute friend. The Drexel guy just could not stand Allen Iverson, a typical type of self-hating Philly sports fan. In any other city, all-time-type players like Iverson and Charles Barkley in basketball, Mike Schmidt in baseball, Bobby Clarke in hockey, and Randall Cunningham and Donovan McNabb in football would wear golden crowns and be met with encomiums at every turn. Not in Philly, at least not among adults who have seen lots of losing seasons. Iverson was just not this fellow's dream, despite game after game when, at 5-foot-11, he sped this way and that for twenty-five points and eight assists.

Ella was torn, because she adored the way our seat neighbor paid her adult attention, asking her opinions and letting her share his nachos. But she loved Iverson. One of her favorite giveaways was the Allen Iverson Celebriduck, a rubber bathtub duckie the team gave out to kids one night, complete with Iverson's signature tattoos on its neck. (We also had the Dikembe Mutombo bobble-finger doll—Mutombo would wag his forefinger after a particularly spectacular block—and that wonderful Eric Snow Globe.) She would vie for Iverson's number, 3, for all her sports uniforms and identified with his speedy-small-guy-among-the-trees persona, which was hers exactly.

Even the girl with the Iverson jersey and knowledge of the difference between a crossover dribble and a jump stop was going to be up for Destiny's Child, for a bona fide rock group was going to be miles past Coskey's usual body benders and Frisbee catchers.

Destiny's destiny was what it was, though, and Ella surprised her mom. Sue must have been a bit appalled, growing up as she did in Detroit, which is almost Canada. Fans there are so polite, they apologize when they trundle down the aisle in front of you with their hot dogs. They never boo their own players. They would never think of howling at or spitting on someone wearing a visiting team T-shirt in the stands, which is de rigueur in Philadelphia. Detroit is the home of Kid Rock and Motown and Eminem. Booing rock stars would be heresy.

Except that when Ella came home and told me about the incident, I could see the Philadelphian in her had suppressed any Detroit genes.

"What was she thinking?" Ella said emphatically. "You come to Philadelphia and wear a Lakers jersey? Then you don't expect a boo. She's got a lot to learn."

I never taught the girls booing, exactly, but I went to games with them telling stories of my own youth. One time, my Uncle Al, a laconic and often dispassionate sort, took my friend Howie and me to a Phillies game. Howie's dad was a broadcaster and often did the 76ers games on the radio. When he took us to a game, we got seats near the dugout. Uncle Al was not that connected, so he resolved to match the offer in a different way: He was going to teach us how to boo.

The drive to Connie Mack Stadium was one pointed lesson.

"This is how you do it: 'Booooooo,'" went Uncle Al, his eyes glowing differently than I had ever seen him, his grin getting so wide it could hardly hold his ubiquitous mahogany pipe.

"Boo," went Howie's and my early attempts. Like New York symphony director Leonard Bernstein encouraging his weaker second violinists, Uncle Al intoned heartier and longer, "Boooooooo! Boooooooo!"

By the time we reached 21st and Lehigh, the corner of the park by home plate, Howie and I were masters. The three of us were laughing uncontrollably but booing lustily just the same, all before the first inning could begin. As the Phillies came up in the bottom of the first, we booed at the moment the announcer read off a name. I am sure even for Phillies fans around us, this was somewhat disconcerting, but the cognoscenti obviously knew that Howie and I, perhaps eleven or twelve at the time, had to be carefully taught sometime.

Sylvia was too sophisticated and meticulous for a mere backbiting boo. For her, even early on, a game was going to have a result, and thus the true fan had to have a record of it. From her first Phillies game in second grade, she saw the checkerboard pattern in the middle of the program and demanded to learn how to keep score of a game. We ended up getting our own scorebook, and she meticulously kept every game with its "E-3s" for an error by the first baseman and its "= 7s" for a double to left field.

Random summer weekday evenings saw Sylvia looking over to me quizzically, which meant mostly, "Are they home, and who are they playing?" When she was young, the Phillies still played at Veterans Stadium, a huge bowl-like place with no character at all and, as my friend Eli noted, weird fried-chicken-like smells around every corner.

The price for Sylvia and me was right, though. The Phillies were miserable, or at best mediocre, during those early 2000s. The Phils apparently just wanted to fill the cavernous Vet as much as possible, so general admission was $10 for adults and $5 for kids. Since a good crowd was twenty-five thousand in a sixty-thousand-seat stadium, we could generally move up fifteen rows behind first or third. She was usually satisfied with a big popcorn and help on her scorecard.

Ella was a little more distracted and had become more jaded. Her boyfriend's father got her into a box for the 2009 World Series, so when I treated her and two friends to a game the next year in the upper deck behind home plate—the Phils are now good, so even that was $28, plus a $6 service charge—I got a harrumph. She demanded an ice cream in a miniature Phillies helmet. For that, I had to break out a ten and pray for change.

The first time Ella had a prime seat was when she was about eight. A friend of mine had access, through his law firm, to one of those boxes along the third base line with about a half dozen folding chairs in it. This was back at the Vet, so it was nothing really fancy, but just in front of us was a similar box with a plaque on it saying something like "The Piazza Co."

Fortuitously, the Phillies were playing the Mets, where the scion of the Piazza family of nearby Norristown, Mike Piazza, one of the best major league catchers ever, was playing. This gave me a Dad moment. I told Ella that the owner of the box was the father of the Mets catcher, and I pointed at Mike, who was doing his pregame wind sprints not 50 feet away from us.

The problem was that the elder Piazza was nowhere to be found. In fact, the whole box was empty the entire game.

"I don't understand," said Ella along about the fifth inning, her countenance falling into concern. "His son is here from New York and he didn't come."

That was probably my initial realization that Ella was going to expect parental spectating at every opportunity, which seemed to be daunting back then but has turned to unparalleled pleasure in the ensuing years. A few years ago, I got a surprise birthday present from Ella, who begged me to unwrap it before everyone else's.

The Mike Piazza desk pen set holds a spot of honor on the office memorabilia shelf.

You know what? I have washed out the plastic ice cream helmet from our last Phillies game together to put up there, too.

The Denouement
Recruiting, Reflection, and Retrenchment

scruffy, power-forward-sized, bluish-gray bull-dog looms over the sitting area by the front desk of the Georgetown University athletic department. He seems to smile a bit at visitors, and you can almost hear him emoting, "Saxe Hoya," the traditional Georgetown cheer meaning, cryptically, "What rocks!"

I am impatient and excited. Ella is about ten offices down the hall, chatting with the women's crew coaches. The narrow hall is filled with posters and message boards and plaques telling of Georgetown successes in the sports whose small offices dot the corridor. Occasionally, there is a shrine to some long-ago star of one of those sports—an Olympian, or near so, most distant memories even at Georgetown.

Still, I look at Sue, who is reading the *Washington Post*, a pleasure of hers since she was an intern there after college and does not get to see that newspaper much at home. She is of two minds about this whole recruiting thing. "If she took some more practice tests and got two hundred points more on her SATs, we wouldn't be here," I know she is thinking. I know she likes the bulldog, though. She is a pet person. She must understand.

I try to break the silence. "I wonder if this is where Mr. and Mrs. Ewing sat when little Patrick was talking to John Thompson," I said, invoking the name of one of the foremost Georgetown basketball players.

"Sit down and don't you dare walk down that hall. This is about her, not you," Sue said and then turned to her cell phone to see a text message from Sylvia. "She wants a long-sleeved Georgetown lacrosse T-shirt."

I am wet-my-pants thrilled by it all. The bulldog. The shrines. The long-sleeved T-shirt demand. Even Sue's disdain, which I take as a façade for her own inner thrill.

By this time, I had written about sports for three decades. The college recruitment process had often disgusted me. Some kid who can barely read the front of a cereal box gets coaches flying in on private jets to fix him dinner and beg for his services, while some 760–740–790 SAT kid gets at most a cheery form letter from the admissions department. I looked at the shrine to Allen Iverson when I walked into the athletic office building. Iverson attended Georgetown for a time before skipping out and joining the Philadelphia 76ers, our hometown professional basketball team. Despite Georgetown's magnificent academic reputation, it never seemed to me that Iverson was the intellectual sort. What classes did he take? Could I see some of his term papers?

Colleges tend to publish the range of SAT scores of the middle 50 percent of their admitted classes—in other words, the lower number is the high end of the bottom quarter and the higher number is the 75th percentile. Ella's initial SAT try fit snugly on that lower number at Georgetown. If she were Iverson or Ewing, in the high-profile basketball program, she would be singing "Saxe Hoya" and learning secret Georgetown handshakes right about now. As a potential coxswain, not so much, but still certainly in the running. Whoever told her about

Georgetown, however she had heard about it, it had almost everything she said she wanted: a city, just far enough away from home, with good international programs and Division I sports, not just to play but to watch and root for as well.

The wait on the somewhat tatty athletic department couch was getting long. I was too nervous to read much of the *Post* and started pacing, though not more than, say, 15 feet down the hall toward the crew office. Then it struck me: My impatience was unwarranted. The longer this meeting went, the better it was. I sat down and opened the *Post* sports pages. Say, where were the crew stories? Shouldn't there be a crew pullout section?

A full forty-five minutes after she had announced herself to the assistant coaches in the spare women's crew office, Ella bounced back down the hall with a face that clearly was suppressing something.

"Need a T-shirt," she said, and the smile pushed out just enough.

To understand my euphoria at even being allowed past the front desk of the Georgetown athletic offices, you have to understand how paltry my own college athletic career was. It was probably mid-November when Jim Schroer—rich, tall white kid from the Indiana suburbs of Chicago—and Spencer Armstead—ghetto-tough, small black kid from Richmond— prodded me to come with them to the first day of freshman basketball practice at Carleton. They were roommates and lived around the corner from me on the ground floor of Davis Hall, the dankest dorm on campus and thus the one filled with jocks—or at least those who passed for jocks in the midst of the hippiedom that was late-twentieth-century Carleton.

"What the hell? How good can anyone be here? We'll make it a blast," said one or the other of them. "Blast" is one of those words from the late 1960s that is so far back on the etymological cycle it would today require a footnote explanation, but at the time it meant that there couldn't be anything better.

"What the hell?" I said back, not altogether convincing myself that this would be anything less than humiliating. I went to my room and gathered up my jockstrap and Chuck Taylors and, walking a bit behind them, headed down the path to the New Men's Gym.

The New Men's Gym was already six years old by that time. Carleton had no doubt tried to find a benefactor to ante up some big bucks and get his or her name on the place but clearly had not found anyone yet. The stadium's name had a sense of irony to it. It was Laird Stadium, after the family of Melvin Laird, the Carleton graduate who was Richard Nixon's secretary of defense and thus the direct target of the ubiquitous Vietnam War protests on campus. Better, so I thought, the anachronistic New Men's Gym than, say, the Spiro Agnew Center.

It didn't take long for me to establish myself as the worst player on the Carleton freshman basketball team. However, the roster had a sitcom quality to it that made me fit in quite easily. Spencer was about 5 foot 6, of which about half was Afro. He got out of Richmond, getting a scholarship to some New England prep school whose mascot was a penguin. Its basketball team apparently wasn't much good either, since Spencer said the team's theme song was "We are the Penguins. Mighty, mighty Penguins. Everywhere we go-oh, people laugh and roll." Jim, his foil, was from the oddly named town of Munster, Indiana, and eventually went to Harvard Business School, befriending a lonely guy in his class named George W. Bush.

Our other starting guard was floppy-moppy-haired Tommy Ferguson, not much taller than Spencer, who was probably the fastest vegetarian in all of Iowa. The best sub at guard was another black kid from Houston, Ronnie Tolliver, who barely ever said a word and was shorter even than Tommy and Spencer. My good friend Paul Stiegler was about 6 foot 3, but his Jew-fro made him about 6 foot 7, and his mellifluous voice made him the best a cappella singer on campus. One of his high school classmates was comedian-turned-U.S. senator Al Franken. Our one sort-of-legitimate player was Stu Alexander, who graduated a year ahead of Paul at St. Louis Park High. He was the high scorer in Minnesota that year and got some kind of scholarship to play at the University of Michigan. That didn't work out so well, so he came back to his father's alma mater, Carleton, where he played with us freshmen because he had to sit out a year of varsity as a transfer.

Things were indeed a blast for me until one practice during midterms. Only four of us showed up—this wasn't Coach K's Dukies, mind you, for students at Carleton actually had to study to stay in school—so we played two-on-two. Naturally, I was paired with Stu, a best–worst sort of thing, and at some point he missed a shot badly. I hustled for it and dove out of bounds, saving it but sliding so far I smacked my arm into the wall, fracturing my wrist.

So I rode the bench the rest of the season. I don't think I would have changed the dynamic, though, since the team had lost every game going into the final one, the traditional game with crosstown rival St. Olaf College. St. Olaf is internationally known for its choir, but to us pseudo-intellectual jocks from Carleton, the girls were beautiful and blond and the guys were tall doofuses. One of us wrote a parody of the St. Olaf fight song, "Um-Yah-Yah," which went in part, "They call us the

Lions. We come from St. Olaf. We're big and we're dumb and we can't spell our names. We go to the Center. We gape and we gawk and we sit and we tawk and we roll on the floor."

Still, their basketball team was bigger, faster, and stronger. Splint still on my wrist, I came out to give whatever moral support I could. Our only real defense was to keep hacking the hell out of the bulky Swedes and Norskis. By halftime, we were already down to seven eligible players, several already having fouled out. I decided I would don my number 20 uniform, just in case. At halftime, Spencer started cursing about something, and our coach threw him off the team, which even today seems both absurd and excessive.

Halfway through the second half, one more of our squad fouled out, but no more were left in foul trouble. With about five minutes left, the coach looked over at me and said, "Would you like to go in?"

I must have looked like Buster Keaton in a silent comedy. I jumped up, my shoulder-length hair bouncing like Raggedy Andy's. I subbed in and, somehow, found myself bringing up the ball. About four steps in, I looked at that splint on my wrist and panicked. With no one on me, I threw a pass toward Ronnie Tolliver but pulled the splinted right arm back too quickly. The ball went directly off it, 15 feet short of Ronnie and out of bounds.

All of this would have been embarrassing, but even in its best days Carleton freshman basketball didn't get big crowds. There must have been all of twenty-five faithful there. I avoided the ball at all costs on offense, until there were only about twenty seconds left in the game. Ronnie stole the ball and sent it ahead to me. I miraculously dribbled it left-handed down the court, a St. Olaf player hounding me the whole way. As I approached the basket, I must have had a flash of those old Harlem Globetrotters games my father took me to. I high-stepped and threw a left-handed behind-the-back pass around the guy to Paul Stiegler, who was himself ambling toward the basket. He deftly lofted it in just before the buzzer.

So my one positive event for the season cut the deficit to a mere 105–53 and prevented us from being doubled by the "big and the dumbs" from across town. Since none of the guys who graduated with me from Cherry Hill West played college basketball, I guess I am still the only one with an NCAA career, such as it was.

The summer after sophomore year, Ella and her friend Kendall, who was on her lightweight boat that year, went to the Stanford University crew camp. The day before the camp, we tooled around the University of California at Berkeley, taking the campus tour, looking at my old haunts from when I was a grad student there for a whole four months before dropping out, and making the obligatory school store run for T-shirts.

We also made an impromptu visit to the athletic office, and the girls chatted for a few moments with the assistant athletic director. The NCAA recruiting rules are so strange as to be silly in this age of multiple means of communication. Until July 1 after the student's junior year, a coach can answer a phone call but not return a phone message. The student can come visit a coach, but it can't be the other way around. There can be e-mail contact but not a text message, which the NCAA thinks is more intrusive.

So when we were there, the assistant athletic director called the crew coach, who wasn't in. She gave us the phone number, saying to try it periodically. We had our lunch, leisurely, and called several times, but always got a phone message. Finished shopping and eating, we just wanted to get over to San Francisco, so we aborted that quasi-recruiting trip.

The next morning, Sue and I dropped Kendall and Ella off at Stanford, where we had a nostalgic ride around campus, remembering where we lived and biked when we lived there ten years before for Sue's fellowship. When she returned at the end of the week to pick them up, Sue phoned me; Sylvia and I had gone to L.A. for a few days.

"Don't let them tell you they didn't like this," Sue said. "They are now being hugged by a dozen, I would say, bare-chested young men at least 6 foot 3. I think I want to be a coxswain."

The following spring, the Haddonfield crew coach gave the junior girls two days off from Easter week practice to visit colleges. Ella made arrangements to go to the University of Virginia, and the coaches seemed receptive in the e-mails. Sylvia came along for the ride, and we got to town the night before, just in time to amble toward the campus for dinner. We stopped at what appeared to be a college hangout and shoved ourselves into a booth. The girls, who had been chatty the whole way down, went quite silent as we waited for our food.

"What's wrong?" I asked, thinking the whole Virginia thing might have turned out bummer-like.

"Ur, blumb, purr, ah," is what I think I heard Ella say, with a stifled grin.

"What?" I said.

"What she said was," said Sylvia with a deep breath, "that these are the best-looking people we have ever seen."

At Stanford, there may have been a few good men. At UVA, there seemed to be an endless supply.

The next day, when Ella called the coach during her morning campus tour, he asked her to come down to the lake outside of town and spend the afternoon at practice. Sylvia and I found ways to entertain ourselves, but mostly we stayed by the idyllic wooded area adjacent to the lake where the team practiced.

This was about the high-water mark, so to speak, of Ella's college crew recruitment. After we had driven a couple of hours toward home, Ella said, "I don't know. I don't know if I am good enough to be on that team."

I'm thinking, well, what the heck is there to coxing anyway? You yell in whatever the goofy lingo they use. You steer the boat. You make sure no one falls out.

Ella was having her crisis of confidence, though, and once that happens, it festers, snowballs, gallops beside you, and sometimes eats you up. The Georgetown assistant coach started e-mailing weekly during the late spring, once even sending a hand-written note. Ella became slower and slower to answer her back. Berkeley was interested, but she told Sue after attending that Stanford camp that California was just too far away. The Delaware coach wrote frequently, and she had never even met Ella; she must have needed an experienced coxswain, eventually offering her a partial scholarship. At Penn, she met with two of the students I had taught in writing seminars there, one male and one female, who had rowed, and they encouraged her. Eventually, the coach asked her to apply for early decision if she really wanted to come to Penn.

Ella hurried up her application there and met with the assistant coach on campus, Sue happily coming with her. The night before the early decision answers were to come back by e-mail from the admissions office, the assistant coach left her a phone message while Ella was still at school: "Be sure to call us tomorrow after you hear," said the cheery voice.

It was Sue's birthday, so she and I were going to the fancy joint in Philly where my cousin was general manager. The owner had just been on *Iron Chef* or one of those reality competitions. Everything seemed glorious: Ella was going to go to Penn and row on the Schuylkill, where we could go a mere twenty minutes away and bask in that old reflected glory.

Except, well, no.

Ella rushed home from school—she had about an hour between dismissal and basketball practice—for the decisions were to be e-mailed at 3 P.M. Unfortunately, when she plugged in her code, the answer was, "Denied."

She called the coach anyway, but I could see the conversation was not going to change things. They had assumed things were going to work out and apologized for what turned out to be leading her on.

Needless to say, it was a disappointment, but Ella rallied. The next morning, a Saturday, she said, "What do you think if I apply to Villanova?" I shrugged and said it was okay with me. "And what about William & Mary?" I was perplexed about that, since she hadn't even wanted to stop there when we went to Virginia, but I assented to that, too.

A couple of days later, I mentioned to her that, oddly enough, Villanova had played William & Mary in the semifinals of the Division I-AA football championships just the night before she asked about them. I had seen them on TV.

As you may imagine, her reaction was the usual teen-to-dad "Duhhhhhh!"

But I got back at her.

"Hey," I said. "It's a good thing you didn't watch the other semifinal, or you would be applying to Montana and Appalachian State."

Duhhhhhh, yourself, Hon.

Sylvia was headed off to a Phillies game with her girlfriend one summer evening after her freshman high school year and, perhaps to get in the mood, found the movie *Sandlot* on the tube to watch a bit while waiting for the ride. She was stunned that I had never seen it and didn't know what it was about.

"It is so you," she said.

She left after about ten minutes, but I got hooked on the film and kept it on afterward. *Sandlot* was made in the mid-1990s, but it is set in 1962 Los Angeles. It is about a group of nine preteen mostly-nerds whose social life revolves around playing baseball on a crude sandlot field. Most, including the adult narrator who tells the story in reflection, can barely play, and none, as it happens, does well at all with girls.

So me, indeed.

Well, yes, um, so me. I would like to think that as a twelve-year-old I was both good with girls and good in sports, but in truth I was not. What I have always been, at least in the sports end, was sticktoitive and inventive. It is no secret that these days, many of the dads whose daughters are good at sports were adequate at best, two-left-footed more often than not. Most of us, though, were passionate about sports, which, in my case at least, got us to push our daughters when they chose to be in athletics to be the best they could.

For instance, I went out for indoor track one year in high school, and there were not going to be many meets. They had one, the Camden County Indoor Meet, inside old Camden Convention Hall, which was either a Works Progress Administration project during the Depression or something Washington had built after Valley Forge. It was just old and drafty and unpleasant.

There was no track inside, just a basketball court with lines for an oval around it. Our coach had not been prepared for a 2-mile race, and he asked for volunteers. Since I was not scheduled to run at all, I jumped forward, even though it was going to mean running in a zillion small loops around the basketball court.

The officials gathered the 2-mile competitors a couple of minutes before the race. Since the track was so small and the field large, the makeshift rule was that if you got lapped, you were out of the race. The last six, since there were six medals, would stay in no matter what.

Within seconds, I had one of my vaunted "Eureka" moments. Here was the plan: I would go out as fast as I could. I would let the other lousy runners like me get lapped, but by the time I faded, I would still be left on the track. That sixth-place medal was as good as mine.

The gun went off, and it seemed like my plan was going to work. I could tell no one else had thought of it, because the first few laps, I was not only fast but first. This was the last race of a long day, so all my teammates were watching, and they were going bananas in the stands, cheering me on.

A mile went by in the race, and I was still clinging to my lead. Others were lapped and shooed off the track. Soon after the mile mark, the wall hit and I slowed considerably. Still, I was confident in my strategy as the legitimate contenders started to pass me. Then, about a mile and three quarters into the race, I was definitely last among those still left. I counted those in front of me. One. Two. Three. Four. Five. Oh, no: six.

I tried to speed up, but it was no use. The leader lapped me, and the official waved me off the track, medal-less.

Dotted around my office are other memories of my suspect, if memorable, athletic career. There is a Xerox of a clipping from the *Carletonian*, our college newspaper, noting the time I scored a try—the equivalent of a touchdown—in a B rugby match against the University of Minnesota in my sophomore year. It appears that I also had a second try, but it was called back on a penalty.

I joined the rugby club because—well, I don't quite remember why. I also don't remember this particular game, which is quite odd, since it was apparently my most stunning athletic moment. Rugby has become a bit more popular on college campuses now, many schools even having girls' clubs. What I recall most, though, is that because I didn't drink, I was an anomaly on our Carleton squad. In fact, the watchword of our coach, Bill Hartley, otherwise a full-bearded economics professor, was, "It is not whether you win or lose but who wins the party afterwards."

We also didn't get a whole lot of fans. We still had Saturday morning classes then, and since I had a chauffeur's license for my campus job as a van driver, I was deputized to shuttle the four crucial guys who had a Saturday class the four hours to the University of Wisconsin for a late afternoon game. We got to Camp Randall Stadium and thought we had missed the whole thing. At Carleton, we played on a hillside in an arboretum—no stands at all. Camp Randall Stadium had, I think, eighty-four thousand seats at the time. For that rugby game, though, if you counted pet dogs and low-flying pigeons, a good one hundred souls were there to watch. For this, I risked our lives driving at breakneck speed.

Up on the third bookshelf of the office is a tattered hockey stick blade. Among the other things enterprising Carleton students induced me to do was play intramural ice hockey. I pleaded that I could barely skate, but they said that was okay. What they really needed were goalies.

The way intramural ice hockey worked at Carleton was that games were played at night, outside on what was known as the

Bald Spot, a slightly depressed meadow in the middle of the main campus quad. The school flooded the area and put boards around a part of it for a rink; the rest would be used for regular ice skating.

Even though Carleton was in southern Minnesota, it got pretty cold at night under those lights. There was a little warming house where the forwards and defensemen went in between shifts, but the goalies stood out there the whole time. The rule was that a goal didn't count if it was lifted more than a blade's height. Even at that, I was miserable. Cold and miserable. Twenty-below-zero cold and miserable.

The general manager of the Minnesota North Stars knew some kid at the school, so he offered to come down and give out the awards at the end-of-season banquet. Most of the awards were real and positive. Not mine. That tattered blade was for the worst player in the league. Cold and miserable and resolutely awful.

I thought I had my athletic retribution, though, when I was made Czar of Rotblatt. Rotblatt was the Carleton softball league, named after Marvin Rotblatt, a neighbor of a mid-1960s Carleton graduate who thought it would be clever to name a league after a guy with such a sonorous-sounding name. Marv was a cigar-chomping Jewish salesman by that time, but for a short stint he pitched for the Chicago White Sox. Every other year, the league transported Marv to Minnesota—he had no other connection to Carleton—to speak at the end-of-season banquet, where we had nothing but joke awards. Marv would tell some off-color one-liners and tales, probably apocryphal, about the major leagues.

As Czar, I coordinated statistics, supervised the early season player draft, wrote the stories about Rotblatt for the school newspaper, made up the awards, shepherded Marv when he came to campus, and got to have an electric Hamm's Beer sign, complete with "flowing" waterfall, in my room.

I also got to play in the hundred-inning game at the end of the season, even though I was as awful a softball player as I was a hockey goalie. There, too, I stood out. By graduation—and, who knows, maybe even today—I held the mark for the lowest batting average in the history of Rotblatt hundred-inning games, a woeful .091.

My own athletic career was one of desperate participation, not college recruitment. That my daughter could take being recruited or not with such indifference was hardly understandable to me.

I had lived the comedy in the arena and reveled in it, but truly, I would have been right there with Joe Hardy, sacrificing my soul for even a lone at bat against the Damn Yankees or a mere moment's chance to yell "Saxe Hoya" with the drunken alumni.

What Have
We Learned?
Where Will We Go?

T he large young men, some exposed, as my mom would say, down to their *pupiks* in their Spandex and others barely covering any exposed flesh in their unzipped jacket-sweats, flexed or promenaded along the banks of the Cooper River. The morning was about as sparkling as it gets in South Jersey. The cumulus clouds looked like painted puffballs, outlining the Oz-like visage of the Philadelphia skyline in the middle distance. Along the north bank of the Cooper, the tents of prestigious colleges and universities were staked in: University of California, Princeton, George Washington, Georgetown. Underneath those tents, the men in Spandex found an array of food choices, mostly provided by doting parents, many of whom had come hundreds of miles to see their sons perform in the 2010 Intercollegiate Rowing Association championship regatta.

It had been four years since I had first looked at this kind of Spandexed young man in earnest. I have lived by the Cooper much of my life. Just across the street, Park Boulevard, from most of those tents was the first permanent home of my synagogue, Temple Emanuel. I still have the commemorative red shovel I got at the groundbreaking in the late 1950s. Soon after that, the county park commission erected a gazebo on a slight rise along that north bank, and I sometimes hid out there while skipping either Sunday school or Saturday morning services. I am guessing during those class-cutting sessions I would look out and see rowers in their shells as they cascaded along the Cooper, but I frankly don't remember. Crew was not then in my blood.

I had come by bike that particular morning, in a bit of a nostalgic haze. It is only 2 or 3 miles from our house in Haddonfield to the Cooper, a rather easy ride to such a fine, almost rural place in the midst of urban overdevelopment. Though Ella had long left the idea of coxing in college behind, I had to finally get it out of my system. Strangely, the NCAA does not control the championships for men's crew, nor women's lightweight crew, so they have their own championships, the Intercollegiate Rowing Association championships, on the Cooper each year.

I followed one of the boats, a men's eight with a female coxswain, to the official tent. She barked them left and right, a 5-foot woman just about Ella's size chirping commands at muscled college men, all more than a foot taller than she. The boat passed muster with the officials, as did the first one Sue and I saw four years before.

The official doing the questioning that day, now seeming so long ago, had smiled at us and asked whether we had any questions. Not really, Sue had said, just that our eighth-grade daughter was going to be a coxswain the next year.

"Oh, on the Cooper," she said. "Oh, yes, she will get a full boat."

Sue indicated that she was pretty sure there would be enough kids to fill a boat at Haddonfield.

"No, what I mean is that she will get a full boat: a scholarship to college if she keeps it up," the woman said. "Coxswains are valuable."

Not valuable enough, I thought, recalling the woman's comment vividly as I slowly pedaled away from the tent. The Cal–Berkeley tent and the Georgetown one were not far from each other by the bridge over the river, a couple hundred yards past the finish line. The grassy area in between was overgrown and a bit scruffy, the county budget for mowing no doubt having taken a hit in the recent recession. Still, when I sidled up to the Berkeley boys, who were to win the varsity eight championship that weekend, they seemed pleasant enough.

"A long way from home," I said rather awkwardly.

"Oh, we like it. It's a pretty river," said one long lad, chomping somewhat open-mouthed on a huge sandwich.

"Yeah, good luck," I said, and pedaled away, remembering the morning when Ella had her first hesitant recruiting experience, talking quickly, while with her friend Kendall, to the Cal assistant athletic director in her office. Kendall ended up eschewing crew in college, too, but sticking with California by going to USC.

I rode slowly over to the Georgetown tent, but no one was there—just a half dozen unattended rowing machines waiting to be pounced upon when the rowers needed a pick-me-up. What would I have said if some coach were there? I wondered. I stared at the machines for thirty seconds or so, sighed, and slowly pedaled away, back away from the glistening river, back away from the Oz-like skyline, back over the bridge, and back toward home.

Ella's junior year in crew was not a particularly pleasant one. Since all the girls were coming back, she assumed that she would cox the lightweight eight that did so well in the nationals in Tennessee again, and they would get better together. Somehow that didn't happen, and each week, it seemed, different combinations of girls were jumbled up in different-sized boats, with little consistency to actually get better. Whatever good feeling had been engendered from the Tennessee trip dissipated quickly, as had success on the water.

The national finals that year happened to be at Mercer Lake, 40 miles north of Haddonfield just outside Princeton, which is the lake where the U.S. Olympic team trains. It should have been an inspiration, especially as Ella and several other girls were trying to be recruited for college teams, but none of the boats did particularly well, and it was hot and sticky, so few people wanted to stay around after their own races to cheer on their teammates.

It was a precursor of Ella's ill-fated recruiting game. When I came back from that bike ride to the Cooper, I was not exactly cured of it all but maybe a bit more sanguine.

Girls do play sports, indeed, but it was time for me to finally realize Ella was not going to do so in college.

The parking lots at the Muldoon Farm in some rural part of western Maryland, dusty as they were on this 95-degree July Saturday, were filled mostly with vans and SUVs with license plates from Michigan to Florida and sometimes even farther afield. There were lots of metal figurines of ponytailed girls running with upraised lacrosse sticks on the back windows of those vans and SUVs, and many bumper stickers starting or ending with "LAX," the approved abbreviation for the somewhat effete cognoscenti of the game.

Maryland is basically Lax Central, one of maybe three bastions of lacrosse—Long Island and northern New Jersey probably being the others—and thus the home of the biggest summer high school–age tournaments for the sport. Sylvia was here as a member of the pre-sophomore 2013 team for the South Jersey Devils, which was all well and good. The real purpose of this and the other summer tournaments, though, was the college recruiting of rising juniors and seniors.

Every sport has its recruiting system these days. Crew, as we learned, is about weekend regattas. College football, baseball, and basketball teams have enough assistant coaches who can view high school games in season, and though there are also showcase off-season tournaments for those sports, the minor sports depend far more on out-of-season club play, when college coaches don't have to be coaching their own teams and can come out and see the players in real games.

This Maryland tournament thing, though, was of a magnitude I had never seen. The Muldoon Farm had been broken up into sixteen lacrosse fields, and several miles away, a mammoth park called the Maryland Soccerplex had two dozen more manicured fields, mowed cross-cut like major league baseball infields.

There were hundreds—no, thousands—of girl Laxers. Devils and more. Ex-treme Whatevers. Super Whosits. Magnifico-Wonderbar-All-Star Lax-o-Mamas. We once followed Ella's sixth-grade AAU basketball team to the University of Rhode Island for a summer tournament, but the couple dozen teams there that day were a paltry lot compared to this.

Lacrosse is infiltrating slowly in South Jersey. Haddonfield is one of several schools to integrate it in the late 2000s. With budget cuts, the school board let it in as a varsity sport as long as lacrosse parents themselves funded the whole enterprise. Our $400 or so a year each provides Sylvia and her teammates with coaches, uniforms, referees, insurance, equipment, and transportation.

For those who think they might want to play in college, though, the high school team is only a warmup. Teams like the Devils and the more powerful South Jersey Select in our area pay the high school coaches from the better teams a stipend and take the best kids who try out, mostly from the better high school teams as well, and put them through a crash program of practices and tournaments for about six weeks in June and July.

It may all sound so grand and glorious, but gazing over the Muldoon Farm parking lot, I blurted out, "With all that I know, what the heck are we doing here?"

The photos of girls' sports in my high school yearbook, the 1969 Cherry Hill High School West Rampant, are clearly of another time. The swimming girls stand on diving boards. The basketball girls have skirts. The gymnastics girls look the most sultry. The star of the tennis team is in white. The cheerleaders have the biggest squad. No one has a name on the back of a uniform.

As far as I know, not more than two or three of those girls in my class played sports in college, and I am willing to bet none of their parents sent them to camps at Penn State, spring basketball tournaments, or anything remotely like them at anything called anything like the Maryland Soccerplex. I would double-down my bet that the largest attendance at any of the girls' sporting events recorded in the 1969 Rampant would not have exceeded the number of girls on that diving board.

Yet I have been to the Maryland Soccerplex and plunked down my "soccer" chair, with the netted cup holder in the arm for my Diet Coke, and gladly watched Sylvia in her #66 Devils jersey (with a red-stitched "Strauss" neatly sewn at the lower fringe), several hundred dollars of equipment attached to or held by her as she and her teammates blow up and down a field far from home.

Get this, too: Despite a dash of requisite cynicism, I have loved doing it.

There is basically this, as well: Often, you just have to live with the system. True, there are landmark changes in all aspects of culture. The civil rights movement was worth getting involved in, for instance. It seems unfathomable that de jure segregation ever existed, let alone in my lifetime, and despite the residue of racism today, I am glad all those who worked for its institutional demise fought so diligently toward it.

So, yes, it would be wonderful similarly, though less importantly, if everyone got together and we all went back to pickup games at the schoolyard and, certainly, fewer parents doing much of anything save letting school coaches coach.

But like Sisyphus and his rock, it is going to take a long string of mighty pushes to tame that mountain.

Even if I looked at it as merely making lemonade out of the lemons that can be the vast all-too-multilayered system of girls' sports, it all has provided me a wonderful bond with my girls, and it even taught them a bit of independence from me.

During the preseason for basketball when Ella was a senior and Sylvia a freshman, the JV–varsity scrimmage for the Camden Catholic game was at home, while the freshman one was a few miles away at Camden Catholic. I thought it would be more likely that Sylvia would play more minutes earlier in the freshman game and Ella, being farther down the bench, would be in her game a little later.

Near the end of the first half of the freshman scrimmage, Sylvia, as usual, ran resolutely to her corner and lofted a three-pointer that swished. I ran to the car and did a few semilegal things to blast over to the Haddonfield gym. Soon after I ran into the gym, Ella took a similar pass and with her signature motion—Sylvia had a classic from-the-front shot, while Ella sort of shot-putted it off her right shoulder—had a similar result, a swished three-pointer. I was reminded in this effort of a major league baseball player named Joel Youngblood who got a hit in an afternoon game in one city, was traded after that game, took a plane to meet his next team, got in as a pinch-hitter in the night game, and got a hit in that second game, too.

Except that Youngblood had a reasonably long major league career, and these were, somewhat shockingly, the last competitive baskets either of my daughters would make at Haddonfield High.

I have never been particularly good at letting something go. I hold on to traditions long after they are necessary, or even viable. I have every computer I ever owned and have had no car, save for one that was totaled in an accident, less than fourteen years. With e-mail, all my former students and grade school playmates are destined to get wakeup messages from me at any moment.

So it is difficult to step back from my athletic times with Sylvia and Ella to gauge what they mean. Somehow, I think they may never be really over, that I will be on the sidelines one day, if not watching their adult badminton game, then giving huzzahs to their sons and daughters.

Both girls have had jobs teaching their sports—Ella in basketball and tennis, and Sylvia in tennis and, strangely enough, golf, when her tennis coach asked her to help out with five-year-olds and their putting. She is actually pretty good at that, and I'm guessing we will long enjoy bashing through the tunnel of the polar bear's legs a few afternoons every summer at the dinosaur miniature golf course on Third Avenue in Stone Harbor. Ella once coached Sylvia's sixth-grade summer basketball team to an undefeated season, and I still grin when I visualize her shouting out instructions in the dress she felt compelled to wear to look "legit." They are both kid magnets, so maybe I will get to see them coaching many mini-Bulldawgs in the years to come.

I don't believe that sports is necessarily the only venue for a daddy–daughter relationship, or even the best venue. It just was our venue. It gave us something to be together at, to talk about, to laugh about. Sports gave my kids a place to be and friends to be there with, but so would orchestra or dance or Sue's vaunted Model U.N. The bigger difference, I suppose, is that there are only a few orchestra or dance concerts, but there are a bazillion-jillion-quadrillion sporting events. The girls and I were with each other more than Romulus and Remus, Steve and Eydie, and it brought us closer.

We had something previous generations of girls and their dads, at least on a mass basis, didn't have. My girls were of the first generation to take sports as a given. As odd as it sometimes was for me to see Ella at age seven or so flying out of her softball cap as something normal, that was what it was for her and her friends.

For that nanosecond after their births when I thought I wanted boys, I believe it was only because I could do sports with them. Two decades out and hundreds of competitions on, the best conclusion is that I could have saved those nanoseconds for some better thought.

On the other hand, I didn't think my girls gave it much of a thought, to tell you the truth, until Ella wanted me to proof one of her college application essays.

Ella chose, fairly courageously I think, to use her essay for Villanova University to tell about how she quit basketball. Villanova is one of those places that is ga-ga over basketball. In 1985, in perhaps the greatest upset in NCAA Final Four history, Villanova beat Georgetown, playing almost perfect basketball to win the national championship. I was one of those lucky folks with a ticket to the game in Lexington, Kentucky, that night, so I should have remembered everything about it.

One summer Sunday morning, though, I was playing in my usual game at the 96th Street court in Stone Harbor, the shore town where we have a house. I am not the best defender in that summer game, which is fairly high level. At one point that morning, I was seemingly hung out to dry as a 6-foot-3 guy was coming down the court one-on-one on me. As we passed half court, one of the guys on the sidelines yelled, "Take him, Harold."

For whatever reason, Harold did not take me. He pulled up from about 18 feet and threw up, in perfect form, a jump shot, which fortuitously hit off the back rim and into the arms of one of my charging teammates for a rebound, which seamlessly took the game back down the court the other way.

Yet in that same moment, it struck me who Harold was, even though I had been in his company all morning, chatting about nothing special and shooting around before the game. He was Harold Jensen, the surprise star of the 1985 championship game. An unheralded Villanova underclassman, Jensen made every one of his shots during the game, essentially making the difference in the matchups with Georgetown. By the time we were playing in Stone Harbor, Jensen was a businessman in Philadelphia, long past his prime, but I guarantee you, had he known I was as paltry a player as I am, he would have surely taken me.

I am sure Ella was wary to let me read that Villanova essay, but I thought it was among her best in the arduous college application process. Though I was not quite a villain in the essay, it was clear that, at least in basketball, I was too overbearing, either outright or subtly, maybe not even consciously. It is not that she didn't love basketball, especially early on, but that quitting it finally, a few days after that Camden Catholic three-pointer, was a relief big enough to emote about in a college essay. I am guessing the admissions folks at Villanova were nonplussed by the topic, but someone must have thought it just contrapuntal enough that they admitted her.

Davidson College has an admissions requirement for a peer to write a recommendation. Ella chose a male friend she had known since first grade to do hers—not her best friend, perhaps, but one who was clearly articulate and knew a lot of insightful things about her. I never read that recommendation, but it was also apparently about her quitting basketball and how her father was none too crazy about it—and how, among the many things that could be a conflict in a young woman's life, it was difficult for her to reconcile with her closeness with her father.

Two years before, Davidson miraculously made it to the round of eight in the NCAA men's basketball tournament and lost a two-point heartbreaker to the eventual winner, Kansas. Like the Villanova championship, that Cinderella run is what often takes up conversation on the campus. Still, despite the recommendation's negative take on Ella's ultimate basketball experience, Davidson accepted her, and because it was a good academic school with a bit of the rah-rah she still wanted in her life, that is where she ended up going to college.

When she got to Davidson, she went out for club tennis, a more social and low-key version of the game. Davidson is one of the smallest Division I colleges, so 25 percent of the student body is a major college athlete. Ella ended up choosing the easier route, two or three times a week, mostly just to stay in shape and meet some upperclassmen.

I have to admit, early on I worried bit about whether her freedom 550 miles away from home would turn Ella into a permanent debaucher. One of the monitors at my gym, a thirtyish guy named Des, moonlights there from his regular job as a counselor at a tough high school in Philadelphia. I told him of my concern.

"You went to every game she played, right?" Des asked me.

"Just about," I answered, almost embarrassed at the thought.

"You couldn't have communicated better, just being there. She knows what you think. You don't have to say a word any more," said Des. "You'll always be in the stands."

When she hit that last three-pointer against Camden Catholic, Ella's foot was encased in what seemed like inches of tape. It turned out that she had a bunion, a gradual deformation of the big toe side bones of her foot. All the doctors we saw suggested an operation to correct it, not necessarily immediately, but soon. She could have finished the basketball season had she wanted, and maybe otherwise she would have stuck it out for her senior year, but the diagnosis settled it. She went in to the coach, who was in his first year, and volunteered to be a manager instead.

Sylvia was another case. She had just stopped liking the game itself and found everything she could to reinforce her decision. A few days after her three-pointer, something happened either at practice or in the carpool home that sliced against the grain. She, too, went to her coach and said that she would be the manager if they needed one, so she kept score the whole year and vowed the next winter to go out for indoor track, both because she had good friends there and to stay in shape for her other sports, lacrosse and tennis. The freshman and varsity basketball coaches tried to convince her to stay on the team, saying that she would play a lot of JV as well, but Sylvia is the not-going-back-on-it type.

She told me later on that in some ways, it was just a trend she feels works for lots of things. Soccer, softball, and basketball were her early sports, and tennis, winter track, and lacrosse were for high school.

"No use getting bored," she said, and I envision her doing rugby and water polo and pole vaulting, or something like that, in college.

Ella had her operation just after midterms, and by that time the coach had asked her to do game filming as the bigger part of her managerial duties. With the stands on the side opposite the benches usually empty, and thus without heads bobbling in the way of the action, she would set up the camera there. I was still going to all the girls' games, but during the first game Ella was filming, I sat as usual with the other parents. Then I noted her up there on the top row across the court alone with her camera and tripod. I excused myself and went over to sit with her.

After her operation, midway through the season, I was not just company but a necessity. The camera battery would often run low, and I would scurry down to a courtside outlet at halftime—and sometimes during long time-outs—to recharge it so she could get it through a whole game. Unless her boyfriend showed up, which happened only a couple of times, she and I were a team, home and away, from Paulsboro to Delaware to that Haddon Heights court where she saw her first game those many years before.

I'm sure the coach winced at times when, watching the tapes in his study, he could hear us criticize some decision or play in our indiscreet discussion of the games. But our time together was unforced company, not so far from that first Haddon Heights game, where I taught her that winning by too much was hardly winning at all.

The Haddonfield girls' team had a miraculous season, and I think Ella was eventually happy that she had a small part in it. Three times during the season, the girls came back from what seemed insurmountable double-digit deficits in the second half. Despite never having enough height or enough speed but always enough grit, they won the South Jersey Group II championship, losing by only ten in the state semifinals to the otherwise invincible champ, Shabazz of Newark.

That game was at a neutral site, at the shore a little more than an hour's ride home. On the way back, Ella and I started chatting about the game, dissecting it as we had so many games, so many times before, whether our objects were the Sixers, our yearly Penn–Princeton game, or tussles long ago even onto Mr. Edwards's 6-foot basket days.

About a half hour in, we were done, and she turned on the rock station, pushing the seat back for a little music-snooze. The boyfriend would be waiting when we got back home, and some goofball reality show would occupy them and Sylvia in the family room, so she needed some rest.

I looked out into the dark night; the Jersey pines seem to ooze blackness on the drive through them from the shore to our home. It only took about a minute, and a tear started trickling down, stage right.

Our analysis of the game, how maybe, maybe, maybe if this or that had gone right, Shabazz could have gone down to Haddonfield, was to be our last little chat of that type.

The clock hand that had started that night in Haddon Heights when we discovered girls played sports, had finally reached midnight. The old pumpkin carriage had given us a mighty ride, and I certainly don't regret a moment of it.

There was still time for Sylvia, though, and maybe having only one would change Dad a little bit, too. Strange as it is, it took a long time for me to realize that I was implicitly asking for the girls to perform for me in their sports. One of the better basketball players I encountered at my gym—he still holds the Philadelphia Catholic League record for scoring average in a season—had little kids and asked me, "So Strauss, what is it like to watch your girls play?"

I told him, "You know, out there on the basketball court, the other nine kids are in black and white, and yours is in blazing Technicolor."

It is never more true than when I go to Sylvia's tennis matches. Sometimes, because of the distance and the time— mostly weekday afternoons—I am the only parent there. This is the state championship team, mind you, with many times a season the top seven players not losing so much as a game among them, winning everything 6–0, 6–0. Sylvia is a decent player, but she's a second-rung kid on this team, mostly playing around fifth or sixth doubles on days like this. Still, there I am, barely a nod at the outstanding kids and bending this way and that with every Sylvia backhand or serve. Perhaps it is no different for the dads of the kids in the chorus of the school musical, or even the Broadway one, but she is my star, and she is really, truly in Technicolor for me.

The girls had mixed feelings sometimes about my obsession with their sporting world, but I know they know I was there for them, as the line goes. I realize that some would castigate me for getting too involved, but a life lived alone is barely a life at all, for the girls or for me. They have made fun of me doing so, and we have gotten a lot of laughs out of it at my expense, so that is worth it, too.

I know I will miss it badly when Sylvia's last lacrosse game or tennis match takes place, or when we do our last Quiz Night at the Pop Shop. Then I will have only my own games to revel in, but I am not Technicolor to me. Sue has always liked my line about fixating on the girls: If you didn't want to live through them, why did you have them? All those games, those matches, those meets, they have been better than if I had been a star and if they were my own, and I am so glad, yes, that girls do play sports.